To my father, mother, and my wife

ACKNOWLEDGMENTS

I would first like to thank my advisor, Prof. Tao Li with my deepest gratitude, for his continuous support and exceptional guidance all through my PhD study and research work. Throughout my time at Florida, I learned numerous invaluable lessons from working with Dr. Li on research, teaching, and life. I joined IDEAL on 2011 willing to pursue my PhD degree in inter-disciplinary area of computer architecture and system. And Dr. Li's profound knowledge and expertise in computer architecture served as great guidance. Without his persistent encouragement and help on solving the obstacles, I would not finish my research work. I would also express my gratitude to Dr. Li for providing me a lot of opportunities with his open mind in both research work and industry experience, which helped me set off my career in a Tier 1 research university. Dr. Li is also a great friend, who always trusted me and encouraged me find my potential to accomplish multiple challenges from both study and life. I would not become a well-developed PhD without Dr. Li's support and help. Thank you for telling me that always keep the courage and never give up, whatever comes it's gonna be alright and gonna be solved.

I would like to thank my supervisory committee, Dr. Sean Meyn, Dr. Xiaolin Li, and Dr. Yongpei Guan, for their valuable feedback and comments. I also would like to thank Dr. Meyn for writing letter of recommendation for me. My lab colleagues are always the best friends and companies along the way. I would like to thank Dr. Zhongqi Li, who provided generous help when I first came to this strange country. I would like to also thank Dr. Ruijin Zhou for guiding me through the first year and helping me to get familiar with my topic. I want to thank Ming Liu for helping me with those hard-core technical problems. You are always the best! Thank you, Dr. Chao Li, Dr. Longjun Liu, and

4

Juncheng Gu, who spent countless days and nights, with me to assemble and tune the system prototype, and to catch the paper deadline. I would like to thank Mingcong Song for working with me to start my network virtualization research. I would like to thank Dr. Clay Hughes and Dr. James Poe II who helped with proofreading in my MICRO paper. Also thank you to Amer Qouneh, Meng Wang, Huixiang Chen, who have supported me in many ways such as experimental setup and proofreading.

Further, I would like to thank my parents, and my wife for their endless love and support to help me become a better person.

TABLE OF CONTENTS

LIST OF TABLES

LIST OF FIGURES

Abstract of Dissertation Presented to the Graduate School
of the University of Florida in Partial Fulfillment of the
Requirements for the Degree of Doctor of Philosophy

TOWARDS EMERGING DATA CENTER ARCHITECTURE
IN INTERNET OF THINGS ERA

By

Yang Hu

August 2017

Chair: Tao Li
Major: Electrical and Computer Engineering

The Internet of Things intensifies the interactions between the physical world and

cyber spaces. IoT establishes such intelligent information connections using billions of

mobile devices and sensors and well-developed communication infrastructures.

Analyzing the IoT big data enables the organizations to optimize their operation

efficiency and enhance their value-added services to customers. However, IoT still faces

many great challenges due to the manageability of a large amount of distributed devices

and the complexity of handling the huge data flows. The enormous amount of data that

generated from distributed sources presents significant challenges to data movement in

existing computing paradigms and infrastructures, in terms of both performance and

expenditures. We explore the current IoT architecture and observe that the

functionalities of computation and communication are decoupled in conventional cloud

and mobile computing paradigms, which leads to an inferior quality of service and the

real-time intelligence in IoT big data era. My two-part dissertation work tackles this issue

by proposing new data center architectures and optimizing the networked systems.

In the first part, we propose "In-situ computing." This novel computing paradigm

offloads the computation functionalities from conventional locations such as cloud data center to a series of renewable energy-powered "in-situ data centers" that are deployed along the data collection paths. By doing so, the computation is converged with communication. The in-situ computing enables the "intelligence-added communication" that provides the faster data analysis at data generation site and lower expenditure. Building the efficient "intelligence-added communication" also poses challenges to current cloud and carrier networking system. The advent of software-defined network (SDN) and network function virtualization (NFV) provides the potential to improve portability and scalability of network function deployment in X86 server-based in-situ data centers. We propose and design a variety of frameworks that optimize virtual network function deployment in both hypervisor-based and container-based NFV environments.

CHAPTER 1
INTRODUCTION

1.1 In-situ/edge Computing in IoT Era

IoT is the interconnection of intelligent devices and management platforms that collectively enable the "smart world" around us. From wellness and health monitoring to smart utility meters, integrated logistics, and self-driving drones, this world is becoming hyperconnected at a fast pace. IoT creates a Big Data problem. The exponential increase in connected devices is producing a deluge of valuable data to store, sort, and analyze. Tremendous amount of datasets are generated from distributed machines, monitors, meters, and various sensors. For example, there are approximately 30 million surveillance cameras deployed across the U.S., recording over 4 billion hours a week. Even a single camera can create hundreds of gigabytes (GB) of data on a daily basis. Similarly, smart sensors designed to monitor a wide area can easily generate several terabytes (TB) of data within a week. Moreover, today's fast-growing scientific datasets (e.g., climate data and genome data) are typically distributed among many stations and research institutions around the world. Such wide-area collaboration on location-dependent data normally requires a routine data sharing of tens of petabytes (PB) every year. According to a recent study by the Gartner Inc., transferring all these distributed datasets to a central location for processing will not be technically and economically viable in the big data era. This explosion of data and data analytics is generating new, more sophisticated ways to redesign processes and create new opportunities.

More importantly, for many data-driven projects that lack broadband access, the data movement issue becomes particularly acute. Some examples include oil/gas exploration, rural geographical surveying, astronomy observing in remote area, video surveillance for wildlife behavioral studies and epidemic monitoring (e.g., Ebola) in Africa. While satellite/microwave based transmission has been used in some cases, it can cost over thousands of dollars per month with very limited network bandwidth.

Rather than constantly move a huge amount of data to a central data warehouse for processing, we instead explore a fundamentally different approach: tapping into in-situ server systems (InS). The idea is to bring servers to where data is located to pre-process part, if not all, of the datasets. For in-stance, these servers can be used to eliminate duplicate copies, compress logs, or normalize data formats. Recently, a similar in-situ data processing scheme called fog computing has been proposed by Cisco to help prevent cloud systems from being overwhelmed. However, it only uses Cisco's routers to process network traffic. The idea of in-situ computing has also been used in the HPC community to solve the I/O overhead for compute-intensive workloads [1]. In this work we repurpose this concept to design server systems that can accelerate or facilitate the processing of distributed raw datasets.

1.2 Network Function Virtualization: For the Network Intelligence

The network is the critical element for IoT implementations. It provides carrier-grade reliability, manages millions of heterogeneous IoT devices, collects vast amount of IoT data, and provides real-time communications to/from IoT sensors. Intelligence must be distributed across the IoT network (from sensor to data center) depending on application requirements. The network should support Mobile-Edge Computing (MEC) and be able to support IoT control nodes distributed at the edge for latency sensitive applications. Some applications require IoT sensor gateways—distributed at edge to filter traffic flooding the network.

16

Network Function Virtualization (NFV) is an initiative driven by the largest service providers (SP) to increase the use of virtualization and integrate intelligence into their network infrastructures. NFV leverages virtualization technology and operates network functions on standard servers to fundamentally decouple the customized and inflexible network hardware. Leading SPs have begun a significant network transformation led by implementations of NFV platforms. NFV and Software-Defined Networking (SDN) provide technology to customize the network to IoT requirements. NFV's ability to distribute computations throughout the network enables near real-time analytics and business intelligence. Today, NFV provides a plethora of virtual network functions (VNFs), including gateways, mobile core, deep packet inspection (DPI), security, routing, and traffic management that can be combined to deliver the customized network services required by IoT. In this part, we tackled the following fundamental and open challenges in achieving efficient virtualized network function deployment on commodity off-the-shelf (COTS) servers in IoT data centers.

1.3 Research Goals

The enormous amount of data that generated from distributed sources presents significant challenges to data movement in existing computing paradigms and infrastructures, in terms of both performance and expenditures. We explore the current IoT architecture and observe that the functionalities of computation and communication are decoupled in conventional cloud computing and mobile computing paradigms, which leads to an inferior quality of service and the real-time intelligence in IoT big data era. My two-part dissertation work tackles this issue by proposing new data center architectures and optimizing the networked systems. In the first part, we propose "In-situ computing." This novel computing paradigm offloads the computation functionalities from

17

conventional locations such as cloud data center to a series of renewable energy-powered "in-situ data centers" that are deployed along the data collection paths. By doing so, the computation is converged with communication. The in-situ computing enables the "intelligence-added communication" that provides the faster data analysis at data generation site and lower expenditure. However, the rural area-deployed in-situ data center poses challenges to the existing data center power/energy management system. We propose an in-situ data center design and build a solar-powered real system prototype. We then move eyes to the power and energy management issues at cloud data centers and propose a workload management framework for the modern software-defined central data center.

Building the efficient "intelligence-added communication" also poses challenges to current cloud and carrier networking system. The colossal traditional fixed-function network hardware severely restricts the network deployment on in-situ data centers. The advent of software-defined network (SDN) and network function virtualization (NFV) provides the potential to improve portability and scalability of network function deployment in X86 server-based in-situ data centers. However, further efforts are still needed to achieve the efficient and high-performance NFV deployment in in-situ data centers. In the second part of my dissertation, we propose and design a variety of frameworks that optimize virtual network function deployment in both hypervisor-based and container-based NFV environments.

CHAPTER 2
RELATED WORK

2.1 In-Situ Computing

Recent studies highlight various opportunities for building more powerful and

efficient data centers, such as thermal control [2], deep sleep [3], peak power shaving [4],

market-driven system [5], hyperthread-aware power estimation [6], feedback control [7],

and reconfigurable systems [8]. While all of the prior arts focus on pushing the efficiency

limits of today's data center infrastructure, we instead explore the opportunity of

offloading the ever-growing data processing burden to in-situ servers. The importance of

developing such a new data-centric system that bridges the gap between computing

capability and data growth has been recognized in different ways [9].

In-Situ Computing: The concept of in-situ computing has been proposed in the

HPC and system research community to solve the I/O overhead issue. Several studies

propose performing data analysis while scientific applications producing data [1] or

moving computation from compute node to storage servers [10]. However, they only look

at in-situ computing within the data center. They can neither solve the bulk data

movement issue, nor address the grand power budget challenge faced by today's data

centers. Several networking research [25] also try to bring computation to the network

edge near data sources. However, these proposals are limited to sensor nodes and

network routers, lacking the necessary storage capacity and computing capability for

handling massive amount of data.

Green Data Centers: Many recent work has explored data center powered by

renewable energy [13-17]. The most representative works are Parasol [13], Oasis [18],

Blink [16], and Net-Zero [19]. However, our design differs from prior studies in both architecture and power management strategies.

The Parasol project includes a group of system design [13, 20]. Its prototype is a solar-powered micro-data center backed by grid-tie and batteries. Its main feature is to smartly schedule deferrable jobs and select the source of energy to use. Our work distinguishes itself from Parasol in three aspects: (1) Parasol mainly focuses on data center level design, whereas InSURE looks at small-scale clusters deployed near the data. (2) The energy source selection strategy of Parasol is not applicable for standalone in-situ servers that have no access to utility grid. (3) Parasol is mainly concerned with renewable power variability, while InSURE mainly focuses on the efficiency of energy delivery from standalone systems to in-situ nodes.

The highlight of Oasis is that it exploits incremental green energy integration at the PDU level for scaling out server clusters. It focuses on adding server racks to existing data centers and therefore is expected to incur the same data movement problem as cloud data centers. In addition, similar to Parasol, Oasis is a grid-connected system that relies on a controller to change power supplies.

Blink leverages fast power state switching to match server power demand to intermittent power budget. The proposed design mainly focuses on internet workloads and lacks the ability to optimize energy flow efficiency.

Net-Zero is a solar energy powered server rack that matches load energy consumption to renewable energy generation to achieve carbon-neutral computing. It also relies on net-metering (a grid-dependent power synchronization mechanism) and cannot be used on in-situ systems.

Energy Storage Management: Batteries have attracted considerable attentions recently due to their importance in large data centers [21-23]. In contrast to prior energy storage systems designed for emergency handling purpose (rarely used) and peak shaving purpose (occasionally used), batteries used for standalone InS often incur cyclic usage, i.e., they are discharged in a much more frequent and irregular manner. In addition, prior studies overlooked several critical battery properties, resulting in sub-optimal tradeoffs for in-situ systems. In [24], the authors investigate a dynamic control scheme for distributed batteries, but it does not consider renewable energy and in-situ environment.

2.2 Performance Optimization of Networking System

Recent studies highlight various opportunities for enhancing networking performance. While all of the prior studies either focus on optimizing the I/O performance on NUMA system or improving the virtual switch performance, our research bridges the gap between networking function virtualization and NUMA-based server systems to provide more flexible data plane flow management.

Thread mapping on multicore and NUMA system. Several research efforts have developed mechanisms that mitigate hardware resource interference and improve the throughput on multicore and multi-socket NUMA systems. Tang et al. [25] develop an adaptive approach to achieve optimal thread-to-core mappings in a data center to reduce the co-located interference. Blagodurov et al. [26] observe the limitation of contention-aware algorithms designed for UMA systems and present new contention management algorithms for NUMA systems. Liu et al. [27] characterize the impact of architecture-level NUMA access overhead on cloud workload consolidation and incorporate the overhead into the hypervisor's virtual machine memory allocation and page fault handling routines.

Networking I/O optimization. Several prior works have been proposed to reduce the networking I/O overhead in the operating system, either in kernel or user space. Among those, Affinity-accept [28] and FastSocket [29] explore TCP connection traffic and improves the packet processing efficiency in Linux kernel by affinitizing the incoming flows to one core. However, they only address conventional network I/O issues in the operating system and avoid providing analysis on NUMA deployment and virtual switches.

NUMA-aware I/O optimization. Some recent works have addressed the networking I/O performance on NUMA-based hardware. Hyper-switch [30] employs a dynamic offloading scheme to distribute packet processing to idle processor cores; this scheme takes into account the impact of CPU cache locality and NUMA systems. NetVM [31] proposes a NUMA-aware queue/thread management technique that keeps the consistency of core-thread affinity of each flow on each NUMA node. However, they did not consider thread dependencies and did not design for HSP-based NFV deployment.

2.3 Performance Interference in Resource Sharing System

Shared Resource Isolation. A plethora of prior arts on shared cache partition, including replacement policies based on hardware support [32], based on software support [33], and fine-grained partitioning [34]. Liu et al. propose an OS design for resource partition for throughput-based applications [35]. Heracles uses a real-time feedback controller to manage the hardware and software isolation [36]. QoS policies for shared cache and memory are explored in [37]. Nevertheless, neither latency-critical workloads, nor network workloads are considered in this work. The Ubik [38] controller addresses the tail latency issues on shared resources by predicting the transient behaviors in last level caches. Several prior arts also address the resource isolation and QoS management via enhancing the memory controllers [39, 40].

Interference/Locality-aware Cluster Management Several cluster management systems take into account the interference and data locality when co-locating workloads. Bubble-up [41] detects memory pressure and optimizes the colocation for latency-critical workloads. DeepDive [42] uses mathematical models and clustering techniques to detect interference in cloud data centers. DejaVu [43] employs VM clone technique to run it in a black box to detect interference. DejaVu also handles new applications and allocates resource according to demands. Paragon [44] and Quasar [45] estimate the impact of interference on performance and use classification technique to analyze the unknown workloads and makes decisions on allocating and assigning resources. HOPE [46] proposes a graph-based cluster power management framework. Quincy [47] is a cluster scheduling algorithm that uses the amount of data transfer as the measure of locality and encodes it into the price model. Then, scheduling decisions are made by solving a min-cost flow problem.

CHAPTER 3
TOWARDS SUSTAINABLE IN-SITU SERVER SYSTEMS IN THE IOT ERA

In this chapter, we discuss a new computing paradigm-in-situ computing. We investigate two representative in-situ computing applications, where data is normally generated from environmentally sensitive areas or remote places that lack established utility infra-structure. These very special operating environments of in-situ servers urge us to explore standalone (i.e., off-grid) systems that offer the opportunity to benefit from local, self-generated energy sources. In this work we implement a heavily instrumented proof-of-concept prototype called InSURE: in-situ server systems using renewable energy. We develop a novel energy buffering mechanism and a unique joint spatio-temporal power management strategy to coordinate standalone power supplies and in-situ servers. We present detailed deployment experiences to quantify how our design fits with in-situ processing in the real world.

3.1 Power Challenges in In-situ Big Data Processing System

Although many of the computing resources today are hosted in data centers, a tremendous amount of datasets are generated from distributed machines, monitors, meters, and various sensors. For example, there are approximately 30 mil-lion surveillance cameras deployed across the U.S., recording over 4 billion hours a week [48]. Even a single camera can create hundreds of gigabytes (GB) of data on a daily basis. Similarly, smart sensors designed to monitor a wide area can easily generate several terabytes (TB) of data within a week. Moreover, today's fast-growing scientific datasets (e.g., climate data and genome data) are typically distributed among many stations and research institutions around the world. Such wide-area collaboration on location-dependent data normally requires a routine data sharing of tens of petabytes

24

(PB) every year. According to a recent study by the Gartner Inc., transferring all these distributed datasets to a central location for processing will not be technically and economically viable in the big data era. The enormous amount of data that generated from distributed sources present significant challenges for data movement, especially when the volume and velocity of data are beyond the capability and capacity of today's commodity machines. Without high-throughput and scalable network, it could take days or weeks to move terabytes of data into the cloud. While the 10 Gigabit Ethernet-enabled equipment and emerging 40 Gigabit Ethernet are making their way into a data center's core backbone network, they are still not widely adopted at the network edge (i.e., near data source) due to high capital cost (CapEx). As a result, Amazon Web Service (AWS) and Google Offline Disk Import now allow users to accelerate bulk data movement by shipping hard disks. Although some third-party solutions such as CERN's File Transfer Service and LIGO's Data Replicator could provide advanced data movement, they often require complex software and dedicated infrastructures, and therefore are only limited to very few scientific research communities. In addition, the operating cost (OpEx) associated with data migration can quickly mount up. For example, Globus, a well-established bulk data sharing service provider, charges $1,950 per month for a 300 TB data transfer limit. As of January 2014, Amazon charges over $60 for every 1 TB of data transferred out of its data centers.

More importantly, for many data-driven projects that lack broadband access, the data movement issue becomes particularly acute. Some examples include oil/gas exploration, rural geographical surveying, astronomy observing in remote area, video surveillance for wildlife behavioral studies and epidemic monitoring (e.g., Ebola) in Africa.

While satellite/microwave based transmission has been used in some cases, it can cost over thousands of dollars per month with very limited network bandwidth.

Rather than constantly move a huge amount of data to a central data warehouse for processing, we instead explore a fundamentally different approach: tapping into in-situ server systems (InS). The idea is to bring servers to where data is located to pre-process part, if not all, of the datasets. For in-stance, these servers can be used to eliminate duplicate copies, compress logs, or normalize data formats. Recently, a similar in-situ data processing scheme called fog computing has been proposed by Cisco to help prevent cloud systems from being overwhelmed. However, it only uses Cisco's routers to process network traffic. The idea of in-situ computing has also been used in the HPC community to solve the I/O overhead for compute-intensive workloads [1]. In this work we repurpose this concept to design server systems that can accelerate or facilitate the processing of distributed raw datasets.

Our interest in in-situ server systems also arises out of the fact that modern data centers are heavily power-constrained, particularly when they employ power over-subscription to reduce cost. In the past five years, 70% companies have to build new data centers or significantly renovate existing facilities to handle the ever-growing traffic. Meanwhile, recent studies are forced to aggressively discharge backup batteries to provision more servers under existing power budget [49]. As data continues to flood into data centers, it is not unusual that the utility power feeds are at full capacity and data centers do not have enough power to accommodate their growth.

A significant challenge associated with in-situ processing is efficient power provisioning for servers running in the field. We find that a standalone wind/solar system with batteries as green energy buffer (e-Buffer) best suits the needs of in-situ servers and demands more attention for several reasons. First, conventional grid-tied designs may not be applicable since the construction and operation of transmission lines are often prohibitive in remote areas and hazardous locations. Even if the power line extension is technically feasible, grid-tied servers can violate environmental quality regulations in rural areas that are ecologically sensitive. In fact, to cap the significant IT carbon footprint, recent studies have already started to harness the power of green energy [13-15, 18, 46]. Further, in contrast to some other generators such as fuel cells and gas-turbines, wind and solar systems have many advantages such as absence of fuel delivery, easy maintenance, and less carbon emissions.

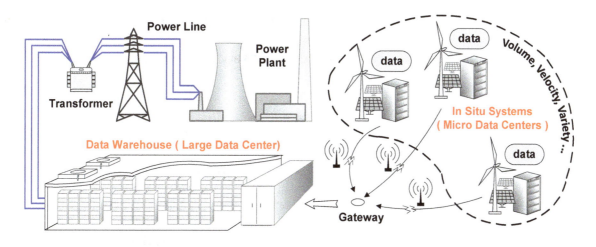

Figure 3-1.   In-situ server system as an ancillary to future cloud.

In this chapter we present InSURE: in-situ server system using renewable energy. As Figure 3-1 shows, we explore the opportunity to benefit from data pre-processing using a group of inexpensive, commodity servers that are placed near the data source. Specifically, we are primarily interested in in-situ datasets that need to be processed timely but do not have a very strong requirement for real-time processing. In fact, it has been shown that about 85% big data processing tasks can be deferred by a day.

Therefore, even if the renewable power output is intermittent and time-varying, we can still leverage it for processing many delay-tolerant data sets.

The main obstacle we face in developing InSURE is the lack of a cross-layer power management scheme that spans standalone power supplies and in-situ server systems. On the one hand, it is important to match the throughput of server clusters to the data processing demand. This allows InSURE users to timely process newly generated logs (so that geologists can use it to adjust their survey strategies) and to efficiently com-press archival data (so that surveillance videos can be stored for extended periods). On the other hand, one must keep a watchful eye on the energy systems that directly support our servers. Without appropriate coordination, one may either lose the opportunity of harvesting enough renewable energy or in-cur unexpected power anomalies. Consequently, it can cause unnecessary data processing delay or even server shutdown.

To overcome the above issue, we have developed a novel energy buffering mechanism and a unique joint spatio-temporal power management strategy that are tailored to the specific power behavior of standalone in-situ servers. They enable our system to intelligently reconfigure the size of energy buffer and accordingly adjust in-situ server loads during runtime. These two techniques provide several key benefits. First, they increase the overall efficiency of power delivery from standalone power supplies to in-situ server loads under varying renewable energy generation conditions. Second, they can greatly mitigate the frequency of server load shedding caused by various in-situ workload triggered demand-supply power mismatches. Third, they also balance the usage of different energy storage units and improve the longevity of our energy buffers.

We have implemented InSURE as a full-system prototype. It is a fusion of modular solar panels (1.6KW), a professionally assembled energy storage system, a Xeon-based micro server cluster, a software management platform built from scratch, and several other components such as internal communication infrastructure, power meters, and micro-controllers. Using our prototype and real in-situ workloads, we explore the technical and economic feasibility of in-situ data processing. We show that the proposed design is highly sustainable and is well complementary to cloud data center in the big data era.

We explore in-situ servers (InS) for managing distributed big datasets today and tomorrow. We present InSURE, an in-situ (standalone) server system using renewable energy, and discuss its essential design considerations. We propose a novel energy buffering mechanism and a joint spatio-temporal power management scheme tailored to the behaviors of InSURE. It ensures highly efficient energy flow from the power supply to in-situ servers. We implement InSURE as a system prototype. We present detailed deployment experiences, demonstrate key design tradeoffs, and show that our optimizations can improve various measurement metrics by 20%~60%. We evaluate the cost benefits of InSURE. We show that it can economically scale along with different computing needs under various renewable energy availabilities.

3.2 In-Situ Standalone Systems: An Overview

The core idea of InS is to provide non-intrusive, eco-friendly data processing to minimize the overhead of bringing data to compute resource in the big data era. This section elaborates the concept of in-situ standalone systems and further motivates our design. We start by introducing typical in-situ applications and evaluating major cost issues. We then describe the properties of standalone energy systems with an emphasis

29

on green energy buffers. Finally, we discuss the importance of smartly coordinating InS and standalone energy systems.

3.3.1 In-Situ Workloads and Cost Benefits

We investigate two representative types of applications that may benefit from in-situ computing: intermittent batch job and continuous data stream. The former normally has large files that are generated periodically (often seen in engineering projects), while the latter faces constant influx of medium-sized data created by multiple machines (e.g., sensor data).

Oil Exploration (*intermittent batch job*): In oil and gas industry, massive volumes of seismic data is collected and analyzed to guide the site selection and drilling [11]. An oil exploration project may involve tens of thousands of micro-seismic tests and each test can generate multiple terabytes of data. Conventionally, these experiment data are processed at remote HPC cluster and usually rely on either expensive telecommunication transmission (e.g. via commercial satellite) or time-consuming delivery via portable storage devices.

Video Surveillance (*continuous data stream*): Surveillance cameras are often deployed in hard-to-reach or hazardous areas to provide an understanding of wild life behaviors, volcano activities, and the source of local epidemics, etc. Many of these projects need a large volume of real-time and high-fidelity data which is far beyond the ability and capacity of conventional video monitoring systems. Conventional solution incurs huge human effort (e.g., manual data retrieval) and exposes researchers to hazard. It also incurs significant data storage overhead and time-consuming data aggregation.

We deploy 8 virtual machines (each VM has 4G memory and 2 virtual CPUs) on four HP ProLiant servers. We use open-source seismic data analysis software Madagascar [50] on 6 VM instances to conduct batch seismic data analysis. The in- situ workload is geographical surveying dataset for 225 square kilometers of real oil field [51]. We assume the seismic exploration happens twice a day and the data volume is 114GB per job. We also setup Hadoop based video analysis (pattern recognition) framework to process video stream data from 24 cameras (1280×720 resolution, 5fps). Details of our system prototype and configuration are discussed in 3.4 and 3.5.

Table 3-1.   Parameters used in energy cost evaluation

Onsite Generator	Energy-related CapEx	Energy-related OpEx
Diesel Generator	$370 per kW lifetime 5 yr	$0.4/kWh (diesel fuel price is $4/gallon)
Fuel Cells	$5/W, FC stack life 5yr; full system life 10yr	$0.16/kWh (natural gas is $14 per cubic ft.)
Solar + Battery	battery life 4 yr, 2$/Ah; solar panel 2$/W	N/A

In both cases, processing data locally is much more cost-effective. Figure 3-2A extrapolates the total computing cost (CapEx + OpEx) based on our real system prototype (detailed in 3.4). The satellite dish receiver costs about $11.5K and the service cost is $30K per month or $0.14 per MB. The hardware cost for cellular service is about $1K and the service fee is $10 per GB. The transmission cost can be several orders of magnitude larger than the cost of building our in-situ system prototype (even when redundancy is deployed). In contrast to transferring all the data to remote data center via satellite, in-situ system can reduce over 55% operating cost if using satellite as backup communication method and 95% if using cellular service. It allows users to save over a million dollars in 5 years.

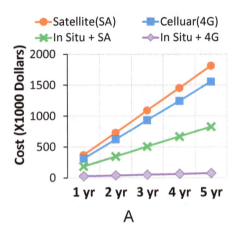 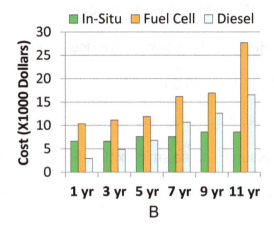

Figure 3-2. Cost benefits of deploying standalone InS, A) IT-related TCO. B) energy-related TCO.

3.3.2 Standalone System and Energy Buffering

Whereas cloud data centers are grid-connected (mostly dual utility feeds), in-situ servers demand different power provisioning scheme. This is mainly because many data acquisition sites are temporary or difficult to reach - they lack established utility infrastructure. Thus, standalone power supplies such as solar/wind system (with commodity batteries as energy buffer) are often more suitable for data processing in field. They can provide eco-friendly energy without the fuel delivery needs like diesel generators or fuel cells do. Such green energy powered standalone systems are also economical. As shown in Figure 3-2B, fuel cell is still an expensive choice right now due to its relatively high initial CapEx. Although diesel generators have low CapEx and OpEx, they are not designed for supplying continuous power and often incur lifetime problems. The main OpEx of standalone solar system is the depreciation cost of energy storage (i.e., batteries). In this work our proposed power management scheme can actually extend their life.

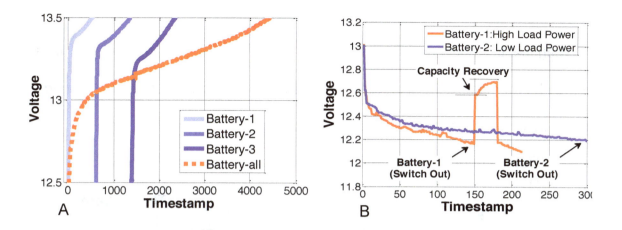

Figure 3-3. Key properties of the energy buffer in standalone InS, A) individual vs. batch charging. B) high load vs. low load.

In off-grid situations, green energy buffers (e-Buffer) play a crucial role in maintaining high efficiency. During charging, for example, concentrating the limited green power budget on fewer batteries is often beneficial. This is because the charge acceptance rate of a near-empty battery is often much higher than a battery that is close to a full charge. In Figure 3-3A, our real measurement shows that charging each battery unit one by one could reduce total charge time by nearly 50% compared to batch charging (i.e., charging all batteries simultaneously). In addition, during discharging, batteries incur super-fast capacity drop at high current. However, this temporary capacity loss can be recovered to a great extent during periods of very low power demand (known as "recovery effect" [52]), as shown in Figure 3-3B. Without careful management, the battery voltage drop can trigger emergency handling control and result in service disruption. Moreover, the aggregated electric charges (Ah) that flow through the e-Buffer is almost constant for a given battery unit before it wears out. This has been verified in extensive test on lead-acid batteries that undergo different charge/discharge regimes [53]. Therefore, one should also carefully balance the usage of the electric charge stored in every battery unit.

3.3.3 The Necessity for Cross-Layer Coordination

When in-situ workloads meet standalone power sources, it is the compute node and energy buffer that link them together. Therefore, it is crucial to judiciously manage both compute node and energy buffers. In fact, this can be very challenging.

Table 3-2. Data throughput of seismic data analysis with the same energy budget (2kWh)

Compute Capability	Avg. Pwr. (watts)	Availability	Throughput (GB/hour)
8VM (High)	1397	57%	14.0
4VM (Low)	696	100%	(Better) 16.5

Table 3-3. Data throughput of Hadoop video analysis with the same energy budget

Compute Capability	Avg. Pwr. (watts)	Delay (minute)	Throughput (GB/hour)
8VM (High)	1411	0	(Better) 0.21
6VM	1050	0.25	0.17
4VM	686	0.5	0.10
2VM (Low)	335	1.5	0.07

First, the intermittent batch job and continuous data stream require different power management policies. Changing the number of VMs assigned to each job or adding other computing resources during job execution are difficult and in many cases impossible. In contrast, it is fairly easy to adjust the VM configuration during the period between two short time windows of the video streams. For some long-running batch jobs, increasing VM instances may not help improve productivity; on the contrary, our results show that it can degrade throughput by 15%, as shown in Table 3-2. The main reason is that the high server power demand can trigger increased number of check-points, causing undesirable service interruption (about 15 minutes for each server On/Off power cycle). In contrast, for video stream analysis workloads, a conservative system con-figuration (i.e., reduced VM instances) may not be wise. As shown in Table 3-3, reducing the number of active VM instances from 8 to 2 can reduce the data throughput by 66% and in-crease the service delay from zero to 1.5 minute per job.

In addition, conventional unified energy buffer lacks the ability to manage the energy flow from standalone systems to InS for two reasons. First, it has to be operated in either charging or discharging mode. The entire battery unit has to be dis-connected from the load once its terminal voltage is below certain threshold for charging (or system protection reasons). In this case InS has to be shut down and its solar energy utilization drops to zero. Figure 3-4 demonstrates this phenomenon on our prototype. Second, due to the very limited power budget in the in-situ environment, a unified energy buffer sometimes cannot receive the highest charging rate even if all the available solar power budget is used to charge the battery. Consequently, offline in-situ servers may incur extended waiting time.

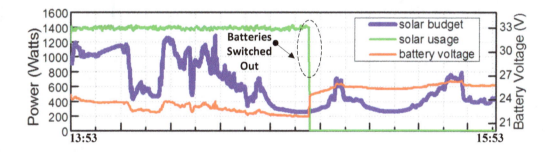

Figure 3-4.   Snapshot of a 2-hour traces for seismic analysis.

3.3 Sustainable In-Situ Power Management

The unique operating environment of in-situ standalone servers requires a new, supply-load cooperative power management approach. In this work we propose InSURE, in-situ server systems using renewable energy (as the primary power source). The main goal of our design is to maintain highly productive data pre-processing and overcome the

35

significant efficiency bottleneck caused by energy buffers. To achieve this, InSURE

exploits two novel power management approaches:

1) Reconfigurable distributed energy storage

We synergistically integrate a power switch network with distributed battery

architecture. It allows the energy buffer to be operated in hybrid modes and adjust its

size.

2) Joint spatio-temporal power management

This technique jointly optimizes the efficiency of energy delivering 1) from

standalone power supply to energy buffer and 2) from the energy buffer to compute

servers.

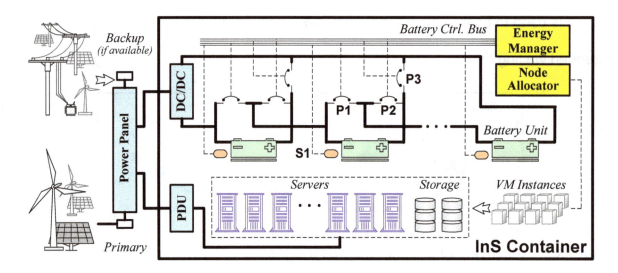

Figure 3-5.   Schematic diagram of InS with adaptive energy buffer and smart node
allocator.

3.3.1 System Overview

Figure 3-5 depicts the full system architecture of InSURE. A remarkable feature of

InSURE is that it has built-in battery array that allows us to freely map a fraction of the

stored green energy to servers. We leverage Facebook's external energy storage

architecture and extend it by adding distributed power switches. This idea is partially enlightened by the reconfigurable battery design in the power system community. As a result, InSURE can reconfigure the size of its energy buffer to optimize the energy flow from supply to load.

The major tuning knobs of our energy buffer are a set of switches managed by a PLC module. In Figure 3-5, three power switches (P1, P2, and P3) are used to manage the battery cabinets to provide different voltage outputs and ampere-hour ratings to servers. For example, if P1 and P3 are closed while P2 is open, the batteries are connected in parallel. If switches P1 and P3 are open while P2 is closed, the batteries are connected in serial. The PLC uses sensors (S1) to monitor the runtime status of each battery cabinet. It further communicates with the VM allocator to enable power-aware load matching.

In Figure 3-5, the in-situ servers and on-site power systems can actually be placed into a modular container. Some major components, such as the server rack, battery cabinet, and renewable power generator are all standardized and highly modular. As a result, the design complexity and maintenance cost is relatively low. If any of the above components requires re-placement, the construction lead time is also very short.

3.3.2 Operating Modes

InSURE supports a variety of operating modes, as shown in Figure 3-6. Based on the state of the energy buffer, we categorize them into four types: Offline, Charging, Standby, and Dis-charging. In the Offline mode, batteries are disconnected from the server load for system protection purposes. In the Charging mode, onsite renewable power, if available, is used for charging batteries with the best achievable efficiency. Our design brings batteries online when they are charged to a pre-determined capacity (90%). In the Standby and Discharging modes, we use renewable energy (directly generated from on-site green generator or energy stored in the buffer) to power server clusters.

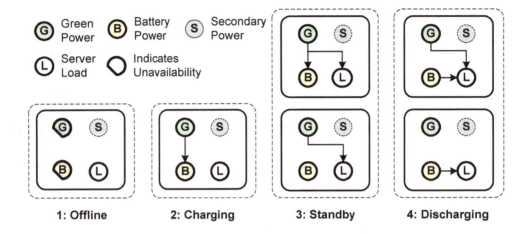

Figure 3-6.   The various energy flow scenarios for InSURE.

The transition between various operating modes is shown in Figure 3-7. Different battery units of InSURE's e-Buffer can be operated at different modes. They can adapt their operating modes to various scenarios based on the stored energy budget, server power demand, and battery health conditions.

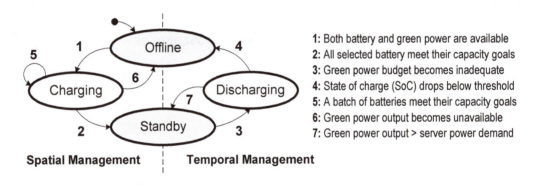

Figure 3-7.   Operating mode transition of InSURE energy buffer.

3.3.3 Spatial Management

The spatial power management scheme (SPM) fine-tunes the renewable energy harvesting (i.e., charging) process for in-situ server systems. It accelerates energy buffering and balances the usage of different battery cells to reduce wear-and-tear.

Other than treats all the battery units as a unified energy buffer, SPM focuses on selecting an optimal subset of the battery unit pool with a two-step control. First, the system selects battery units from the current energy storage pool based on the history usage record of each battery unit. Afterwards, it determines the optimal number of battery units for charging based on the available renewable power budget.

During runtime, InSURE maintains a battery discharge history table and monitors the state-of-charge (SoC) of each battery unit, as shown in Figure 3-8. At each time stamp T, the energy manger calculates a discharge threshold δ_D, which specifies the upper bound of the aggregated total discharge. Assuming that the lifetime discharge is D_L, the unused discharge budget in the last control period is D_U, and the desired battery lifetime is T_L, the discharge threshold is given by (3-1).

$$\delta_d = D_U + T\!\!\Big/_{\!T_L} \cdot D_L \qquad\qquad (3\text{-}1)$$

Requires: The usage statistics $AhT[i]$ of each battery unit i, designated total discharge D_L, desired lifetime T_L, and previously unused budget D_U

1: **For** each beginning of a coarse-grained control interval T
2:          Update the upper limit of   battery discharge $\delta_D = D_U + D_L \cdot T/T_L$
3: **For** each battery cabinet i in the *offline group*
4:          Move i into *charging group* **If** $AhT[i] < \delta_D$

Figure 3-8.　Spatial management scheme in the Offline mode.

We use the above threshold as the default criterion for determining whether a battery unit is over-used. Batteries are put into offline group if their aggregated discharge is greater than the threshold value. After the first screening, we obtain a group of battery that can be used in the incoming cycle.

In the second step, our system calculates the charging rate based on the available renewable power budget, as shown in Figure 3-9. If renewable power is inadequate, our system will reduce the number of battery units in the following round of batch charging. By concentrating the precious renewable power to fewer battery units, we could maintain a near-optimal charge rate in different renewable power generation levels. Once all the selected batteries are charged to a pre-determined level, they will be connected to the server cluster. In the Standby mode, batteries receive float charging.

Requires: The estimated green power budget P_G in the following battery charging period; the peak charging power P_{PC}

1:	Calculate the optimal number for batch charging $N = P_G/P_{PC}$
2:	**While** *charging group* has uncharged battery cabinets
3:	Select a batch of up to N cabinets C_N from *charging group*
4:	**While** current C_N capacity < 90% of its nominal capacity
5:	**Continue** charging
6:	Mark all batteries in B_N as charged
7:	Move battery cabinets from *charging group* to *standby group*

Figure 3-9.   Spatial management scheme in the Charging mode.

The SPM also offers the flexibility to temporarily trades off battery lifetime for better data processing throughput. It may gradually increase the battery discharge threshold instead of using a rigid value. If we use a fixed discharge threshold as calculated in (3-1), it is possible that only a small number of batteries can be selected during a long period of high server power demand or low renewable power generation. By adding additional battery units to the already selected battery set, we can provide on-demand processing acceleration for a short period of time without significantly affecting battery life.

3.3.4 Temporal Management

To achieve continuous productivity, one needs to make the best use of the stored renewable energy. High-current dis-charging drains the battery quickly, but resulting in very limited energy delivery. Appropriate load power capping allows us to maintain a favorable amount of usable (online) battery units and avoids service disruption caused by data inrush. We use a temporal power management (TPM) scheme to improve the discharging effectiveness of batteries. The main idea is to allow the battery to partially recover its capacity during discharging period by reducing power demand.

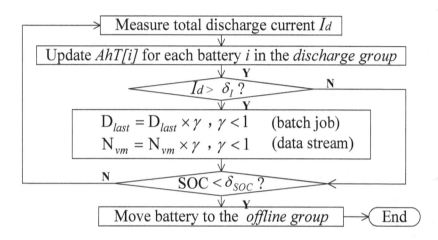

Figure 3-10.   Flow chart of InSURE temporal power management.

As shown in Figure 3-10, our system checks the server load level and the discharging current of online battery units at the beginning of each control period. If the discharge current is larger than a predefined threshold, our system will notify the server rack to cap power. For batch jobs, it will receive a duty cycle that specifies the percentage of time a server rack is allowed to run at full speed. Then the OS can use dynamic voltage and frequency scaling (DVFS) to adjust server speed based on the duty cycle. For data stream workloads that can be split into multiple small jobs, our system adjusts the number of VMs assigned to each job. In the mean-time, InSURE also monitors the state-of-charge (SOC) of battery. When the battery units indicate low energy reserve, our system can temporarily shut down servers (VM states saved).

It is worth pointing out that the novelty of InSURE is not "distributed battery", but a new battery-aware energy flow management scheme for in-situ systems. Prior data center battery designs are only optimized under loose power budget constraints (i.e., with continuous utility power as backup) and does not consider the power variability in in-situ environment.

3.4 System Implementation

We have implemented InSURE as a three-tier hierarchical sys-tem, as shown in Figure 3-11. Its main functionalities are achieved through three modules built from scratch: (1) a reconfigurable battery array, (2) a real-time monitoring module, and (3) a supply-load power management node.

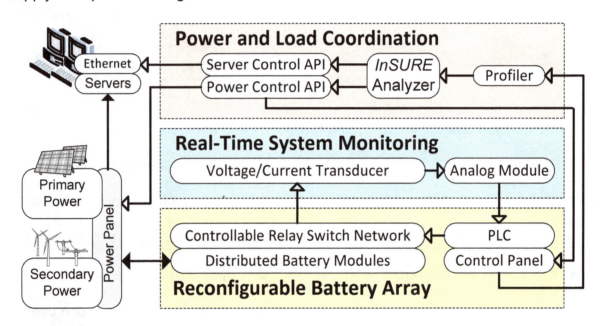

Figure 3-11.   The structure of our verification platform.

Figure 3-12 shows our full-system prototype of InSURE. We deploy four HP ProLiant rack-mounted servers (dual Xeon 3.2GHz processors with 16G RAM and 500G SAS HDD). The peak power demand of each server is around 450W and the idle power is about 280W. Table 3-4 summarizes the technical data of several major hardware components used in our system.

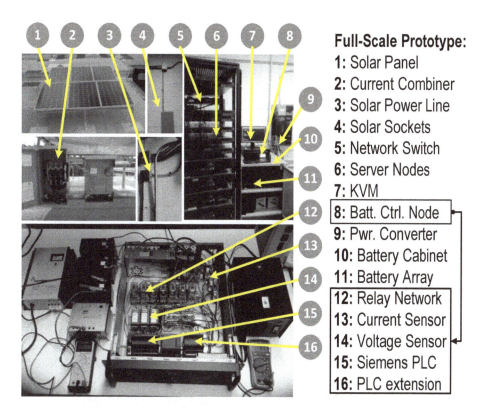

Full-Scale Prototype:
1: Solar Panel
2: Current Combiner
3: Solar Power Line
4: Solar Sockets
5: Network Switch
6: Server Nodes
7: KVM
8: Batt. Ctrl. Node
9: Pwr. Converter
10: Battery Cabinet
11: Battery Array
12: Relay Network
13: Current Sensor
14: Voltage Sensor
15: Siemens PLC
16: PLC extension

Figure 3-12.   A full-system implementation of InSURE. Photo courtesy of Yang Hu.

Table 3-4.   Hardware configuration

PROGRAMMABLE LOGIC CONTROLLER
Siemens S7-200 CPU224 PLC control module, 6ES7-214-1AD23-0XB0

PLC ANALOG INPUT MODULE
Siemens S7-200 6ES7-231-0HC22-0XA0, with 4 way analog signals input

NETWORK & COMMUNICATION INTERFACE
Cisco SRW2024 Gigabit Switch and   Weintek MT8050i control panel

RECONFIGURABLE BATTERY ARRAY
Six UPG UB1280 12V 35AH batteries; Six IDEC RR2P 24VDC relays

BATTERY SENSOR
CR Magnetics CR5310 voltage transducer (In: 0-50V DC; Out: +/- 5V DC) HCS 20-10-AP-CL current transducer (In:+/-10A DC; Out: +/-4 V DC)

SOLAR POWER SYSTEM
Grape Solar PV panels. Total installed capacity 1.6KW

Reconfigurable Battery Array

Our customized battery system uses six 12V lead-acid batteries and a relay network. We use six 10A/24V DC relays as the power switches for reconfiguring the battery array. Each battery is managed independently using a pair of two relays (charging and discharging switch). These relays provide satisfactory mechanical life (10M cycles) and fast switching (25ms), and are ideal candidates for managing battery in our study.

We use a Siemens S7-200 CPU224 PLC module as the controller for our reconfigurable battery system. Its digital output is connected to the relay network and can energize or de-energize the coil of relay to perform battery switching.

Real-Time System Monitoring

The monitoring module detects the battery status and notifies the system whenever the battery configuration profile changes. It also collects key parameters such as charging and discharging current and battery terminal voltage.

To enable real-time monitoring, each battery in the system is equipped with a voltage transducer and a current transducer. Their outputs are further sampled by two analog input PLC extension modules that are coordinated by the central PLC. All the analog readings processed by the analog input module are stored in specific registers in the PLC.

We use an external control panel to link the battery system and the coordination node. The control panel communicates with the coordination server node via Ethernet using the Modbus TCP protocol, a widely used communication protocol for industrial electronic devices due to robustness and simplicity. We design corresponding encoding/decoding components to handle the data communication in our system.

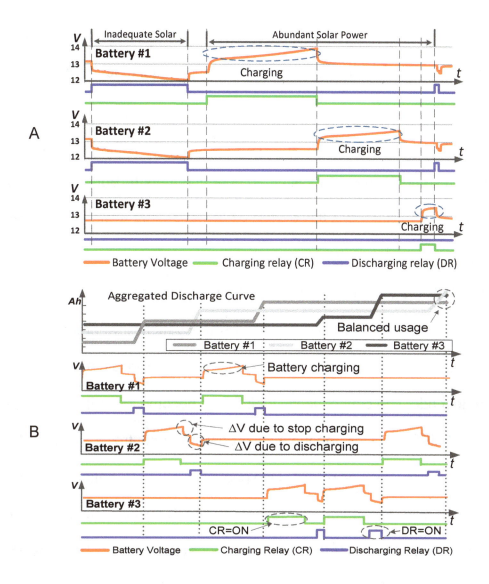

Figure 3-13.   Demonstration of InSURE power behaviour, A) from solar panel to e-Buffer (fast charging). B) from e-Buffer to InS (discharge balancing).

Power and Load Coordination

The top hierarchy of our design consists of a power and load coordination module. This module is implemented on a separate server node. It maintains runtime profiling data of the battery array and performs appropriate supply-load control.

We have designed a power supply switching API and a server control API. The former API provides necessary communication interface that allows the system to select its power source during runtime. The latter API is used to adjust server power demand through frequency scaling, server power state control, and virtual machine migration.

Power Behavior Demonstration

As mentioned earlier, the crux of our system is to maintain smooth and efficient energy delivery from standalone power system to energy buffers (e-Buffer) and finally to in-situ servers. Figure 3-13 illustrates the system power behaviors using our recorded battery voltage traces and relay status logs.

Figure 3-13A illustrates how our design performs timely solar energy harvesting. Initially, batteries #1 and #2 are both fully charged (Standby mode), whereas battery #3 is in low state of charge (SOC). As solar energy generation decreases, batteries #1 and #2 enter Discharge mode, and consequently their SOCs become lower than battery #3. At the time when InSURE receives adequate solar power, our controller starts to charge the battery array based on two principles: 1) give priority to low-SOC batteries if there are multiple batteries that have enough discharge budget, and 2) concentrate solar energy on fewer batteries for fast charging. In Figure 3-13B, our system selects batteries #1 and #2 since they have lower SOC (indicated by their terminal voltage). Our system starts to charge battery #3 after charging batteries #1 and #2 successively.

Figure 3-13A shows how our design manages the green energy flow from solar panel to e-Buffer with balanced battery usage. Initially, all three battery units are in Offline mode (discharged). When there is additional solar energy budget, our system selects batteries that have low aggregated total usage (Ah) for charging. Once reaching a pre-defined state of charge, the selected batteries will be put into Standby mode.

3.5 Experimental Methodology

We evaluate our design with both well-established micro benchmarks and real-world in-situ applications. Table 3-5 summarizes the workloads used in our experiments.

Micro Benchmarks: We use micro benchmarks to evaluate the power management effectiveness. We choose three benchmark programs from PARSEC [54], two from Hibench [55], and one from CloudSuite [56]. They cover a variety of in-situ data processing scenarios. For example, the dedup kernel represents data deduplication, which is the mainstream method to compress data; vips and x264 are widely used image processing and video processing benchmarks; wordcount and bayesian are text-file processing programs (mimic the behaviors of log processing and analysis); the graph-analytic is a data mining application that uses a Twitter dataset with 11 million user data as input. Each workload is executed iteratively in our experiment.

In-Situ Applications: We also designed two case studies using representative in-situ applications on our prototype: 1) seismic data analysis (velocity analysis on 3D reflection seismic survey) widely used in the oil industry; and 2) video surveillance analysis (pattern recognition based video processing) for today's widespread surveillance cameras. The former workload is batch processing with a data rate of 114GB per job, two jobs a day. The latter is continuous data stream analysis based on videos generated from 24 cameras (0.21G/minute).

We host all workloads in virtual machines (VM) on Xen 4.1.2 hypervisor. Each physical machine (PM) hosts 2 VMs. Normally the first PM is turned on at 8:30AM, and the fourth PM is turned on 11:30AM. Starting from 4:00PM the first PM needs to be turned off and all PMs are shut down usually after 6:30PM. Our system automatically collects various log data and can initiate dynamic frequency scaling (DFS) on each PM. When solar power budget is inadequate, our system can further make checkpoint and all VM states are saved.

Table 3-5.   The evaluated benchmarks and in-situ workloads

Workload		Input Size	Description
Micro benchmarks	**dedup**	672 M	Data deduplication
	graph	1.3 G	Graph analytics
	bayesian	2.4 G	Hadoop benchmark
	wordcount	1.0 G	Hadoop benchmark
	vips	2662x5500 pixels	Image processing
	x264	30fps/640x360 pixels	H.264 video encoding
In-Situ Apps.	**seismic analysis**	114G batch job; collected twice a day	Geo surveying data from 225 km^2 oil field
	video surveillance	5fps/1280x720 pixels 0.21G/min data rate	surveillance video generated from 24 cameras

The time-varying nature of solar energy makes it difficult to compare different groups of experiments directly. Similar to [13], for micro benchmarks, we reproduce our experiments via collected real solar power traces and monitored workload runtime data. Note that we use this methodology only for comparing the optimization effectiveness of our spatio-temporal power management scheme with conventional designs.

As shown in Figure 3-14, we use two solar power traces that have different power variability patterns and average power generation levels. Our traces are collected from our roof-mounted solar panels that use a maximum power point tracking system to maximize its generation. We use daytime solar power traces collected from 7:00AM to 8:00 PM. The average power budget is 1114W for the high solar generation trace and 427W for the low solar generation trace. We use the dynamic solar power budget traces to precisely control our battery charger, so that the stored energy and the consumed green energy reflects the actual solar power supply across multiple experiments.

48

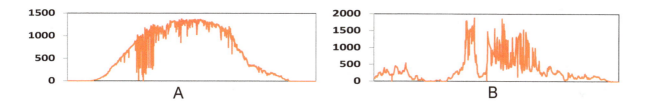

Figure 3-14.   Solar traces for evaluating micro benchmarks, A) High solar generation. B) Low solar generation.

3.6 Results and Deployment Experiences

We start by analyzing the system behaviors of InSURE using real traces and system logs obtained from our prototype. We then evaluate our spatio-temporal power management scheme using micro-benchmarks. Finally, we evaluate InSURE using real in-situ workloads and discuss its cost benefits.

3.6.1 System Trace Analysis

To understand the power behavior of inSURE. We investigate a typical system power trace collected from prototype, as shown in Figure 3-15. We mark five typical regions (Regions A~D) that frequently appear in our everyday operation. Our standalone in-situ system starts to charge a selected subset of batteries in the morning, as shown in Region-A. During this period, the battery voltage gradually increases until it reaches a preset value. Then the system enters standby mode.

Figure 3-15 also shows a zoom-in view of a fraction of the system trace. As we can see, Region-B incurs a great deal of solar usage surges. This is because our system uses a Perturb and Observe (P&O) peak power tracking mechanism [57]. Our maximum power point tracker (MPPT) has built-in sensors that can identify if we have reached the optimal solar power output. To reach this point, the controller increases server load tentatively. This is reflected as many green peaks in Region-B.

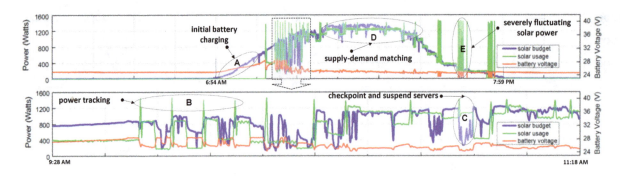

Figure 3-15. Solar power budget trace and battery state of charge (as indicated by voltage) collected using our monitors and sensors.

Region-C shows the temporal control of our system. In this region, the load power demand is significantly larger than the maximum solar budget, and battery is in discharging mode. When our system realizes that the discharge current is unsafe, it triggers power capping (VM check-pointing and server shutdown in this case). As a result, the solar power demand of our in-situ system drops at the end of this region.

The Region-D is the most desirable region. Renewable power is adequate and system can harvest the maximum benefit from renewable energy powered data-preprocessing. In contrast, Region-E is an unfavorable region as severely fluctuating power budget can cause many supply-load power mismatches. Using peak power capping may solve this issue.

3.6.2 System Log Analysis

We further investigate InSURE by looking at the detailed system logs. In Table 3-6 we show a few key values that we extracted from three pairs of day-long operation logs (two sunny days, two cloudy days, and two rainy days). Each pair of traces has the same total solar energy budgets and very similar power variability patterns. We experiment with two power management schemes: 1) spatio-temporal optimization (Opt), and 2) aggressively using energy buffer (No-Opt).

50

Our results demonstrate a key trade-off in in-situ standalone server system design, i.e., the efficiency of the energy buffer can be improved at the expense of less renewable energy utilization. As Table 3-6 shows, the effective energy us-age does not equal to the overall load energy consumption. This is because VM checkpointing operations and the on/off power cycles of servers consume large amount of energy but stall data processing progress. Since the optimized power management scheme (Opt) results in more VM operations and server on/off cycles, it yields lower effective energy usage, about 86% of a non-optimized scheme (No-Opt).

Table 3-6.   Statistics of several key variables collected from the log

		Load kWh Usage	Effective kWh Usage	Power Ctrl. Times	On/Off Cycles	VM Ctrl. Times	Minimum Battery Volt.	End of Day Voltage	Battery Volt. σ	Others in Common
Sunny (7.9 kWh)	Non-Opt.	6.7 kWh	6.4 kWh	12	8	8	23.6	25.2	1.05	Operating duration =11 hours;
	Opt.	6.5 kWh	5.9 kWh	47	16	42	23.7	25.5	0.93	VM mgmt. overhead = 5 min;
Cloudy (5.9 kWh)	Non-Opt.	5.5 kWh	5.2 kWh	10	8	15	23.3	25.2	1.03	Battery initial voltage = 25.4V;
	Opt.	5.0 kWh	4.2 kWh	51	20	51	23.2	25.3	0.92	Battery max voltage=28.8 V; Server pwr. consumption= 350
Rainy (3.0 kWh)	Non-Opt.	2.8 kWh	2.5 kWh	10	8	11	23.3	25.0	1.04	W;
	Opt.	2.6 kWh	2.1 kWh	33	15	38	23.3	25.4	0.93	Max total server number = 4;

Table 3-7.   Comparison of a legacy high performance server node to a state-of-the-art low-power server node

	Data Size	Server Type	Exe. Time	Avg. Power	Data Processed per Unit of Energy per Node
dedup	2.6G	Xeon 3.2G	97s	360W	277G/kWh
		Core i-7	48s	46W	4.4T/kWh
x264	5.6M	Xeon 3.2G	4.6s	350W	12.4G/kWh
		Core i-7	4.7s	42W	101.3G/kWh
bayes	4.8G	Xeon 3.2G	439s	356W	111G/kWh
		Core i-7	662s	42W	621G/kWh

In fact, our spatio-temporal optimization trades off effective energy usage for good reasons. It improves the overall service life (the entire expected lifespan, typically 4 to 5 years for lead-acid batteries) of the e-Buffer and the average stored energy level by avoiding aggressive battery usage. As Table 3-6 shows, the standard deviation of battery terminal voltage of a non-optimized scheme is 12% higher than our design.

Table 3-7 compares the impacts of integrating heterogeneous servers in our InSURE platform. We evaluate three types of workload: data deduplication, video processing, and data analysis application. An interesting observation is that, although emerging low-power servers (e.g. Intel Core i-7-2720 series) do not always guarantee the fastest immediate data processing speed, it contributes to significant energy efficiency improvement on our InSURE platform. They show better performance per watt and incur fewer On/Off power cycles (less overhead). Consequently, by using low-power servers, InSURE can improve data throughput by 5X~15X. In the future, we expect in-situ systems will benefit from more energy proportional designs being adopted by commodity server vendors.

3.6.3 Power Management Effectiveness

We first evaluate the power management effectiveness of InSURE using various micro benchmarks. Our baseline is a solar-powered in-situ system without the proposed spatio-temporal power management. Figures 3-16~18 show the results.

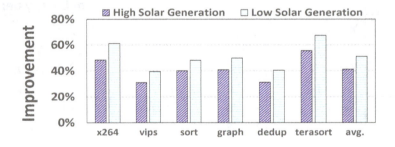

Figure 3-16.   In-situ service availability.

Our results demonstrate that InSURE can significantly improve the service availability of in-situ systems. Due to the optimized energy flow (from standalone systems to in-situ servers), InSURE shows 41% higher service availability under high solar generation. In Figure 3-16, when the solar energy generation is low, the improvement can reach 51%.

InSURE also saves the precious renewable energy stored in the e-Buffer throughout its operation. We refer to the average energy level of our e-Buffer as energy availability. In Figure 3-17, our system shows 41% more energy availability compared to our baseline. This can greatly improve the emergency handling capability of in-situ systems. The improvement is mainly a result from fast battery charging and smart load allocation that eliminates quick e-Buffer capacity drop.

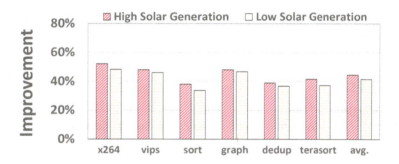

Figure 3-17.   E-Buffer energy availability.

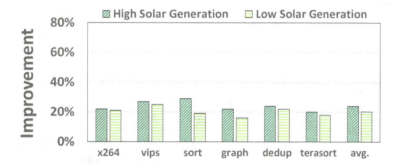

Figure 3-18.   Expected e-Buffer service life.

We also expect a service life improvement of 21~24%, as shown in Figure 3-18. InSURE increases e-Buffer lifespan since it applies discharge capping and balancing across battery cabinets. Note that our optimization is conservative as we allow InSURE to occasionally use more stored energy than the pre-determined threshold. By setting a more restrictive budget, one can further extend battery lifetime but may incur slight performance degradation. Exploring this tradeoff is our future work.

3.6.4 Full System Evaluation

We compare InSURE to a baseline in-situ design that adopts the power management approach of today's grid-connected green data centers [13, 18]. While our baseline system shaves peak power demand and tracks variable renewable energy, it can neither reconfigure its energy buffers nor adapt its nodes to the off-grid power supply. Figures 3-19 and 3-20 show the results obtained from our prototype.

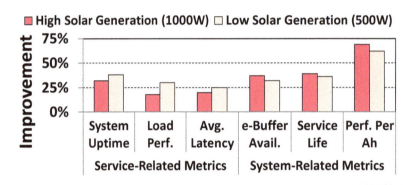

Figure 3-19.   Results of in-situ batch job.

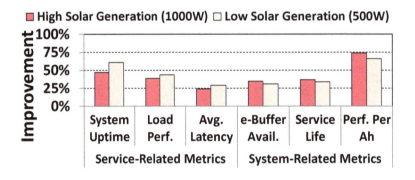

Figure 3-20.   Results of in-situ data stream.

Overall, InSURE outperforms our baseline significantly (from 20% to over 60%) in terms of system uptime, data throughput, response time, energy availability, battery lifetime, and performance per Ah (defined as the total data processed per ampere-hour electricity flows through the e-Buffer).

A major observation is that the energy budget level could affect various optimization measurement metrics differently. In Figures 3-19 and 3-20, we broadly categorize these metrics into two types: service-related metrics and system-related metrics. The service-related metrics are more related with the user experiences and the system-related metrics mainly evaluates the energy efficiency and resiliency of in-situ systems.

The optimization effectiveness of InSURE on server-related metrics becomes greater when the solar energy is lower. In other words, the benefit of our joint spatio-temporal power management actually increases when the standalone in-situ system becomes heavily energy-constrained. The main reason behind this is that the charging process of our baseline system can be very lengthy when solar power budget is low. In addition, InSURE can reduce the significant energy overhead due to increased check points that are incurred by our baseline system.

When the solar energy is abundant, InSURE exhibits greater optimization results on system-related metrics. In fact, both InSURE and our baseline tend to deploy more compute instances and increase its charge and discharge frequency when the solar panel output is high. Due to a lack of intelligent discharge capping and balancing, the e-Buffer can be the major efficiency bottleneck of our baseline system.

The effectiveness of our temporal-spatial power management on system-related metrics is largely orthogonal to workload types. We observe that most of the performance statistics of seismic data are very close to video surveillance. In contrast, the service related metrics are normally workload dependent.

Our results also imply that InSURE could maintain its optimization effectiveness for in-situ systems that intend to over-subscribe their standalone power systems to reduce cost. In Figures 3-19 and 3-20, the height difference between the two bars (i.e., High Solar Generation and Low Solar Generation) is relatively small – less than 15% on average. Even if we cut the solar power budget in half in the Low Solar Generation scenario, it still shows very impressive overall improvement.

3.6.5 Cost Benefits

Although additional costs are added due to the inclusion of on-site renewable power supply, InSURE still provides competitive cost effectiveness. Take our full-system prototype (1.6kW) as an example, the solar array and inverter only account for 8% of the total annual depreciation cost, as shown in Figure 3-21.

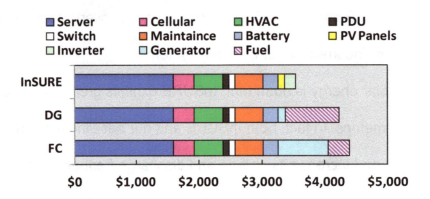

Figure 3-21.   Annual depreciation cost.

The cost of our e-Buffer (210Ah) is approximately 9% of InSURE. However, if powered by diesel generator, the same in-situ servers would require 20% additional equipment and fuel cost, not to mention that it increases the carbon footprint of in-situ servers. For fuel-cell based InS, it can generate carbon-neutral electricity with relatively cheaper fuels but the high capital cost of fuel cell stack has become the main design issue. Compared to InSURE, a fuel cell based InS can increase the cost by 24%. The maintenance cost is estimated to be 12% of InSURE. It is worth pointing out that the data transmission cost in rural areas can be several orders of magnitude larger than the cost of building InS. Adding hardware redundancy result in negligible cost increase but can further reduce maintenance cost. In addition, one can also leverage software fault-tolerant mechanisms to further reduce the maintenance cost.

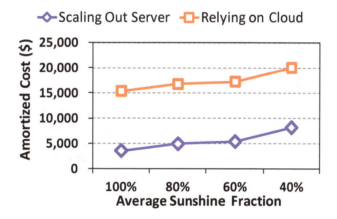

Figure 3-22.   Total cost for scale-out based approach and cloud-based approach (i.e., sending data to cloud).

Another advantage of InSURE is that it can economically scale along with different data processing needs, allowing for wide deployment. In places that have lower solar energy resources (e.g., indicated by sunshine fraction, the percentage of time when sunshine is recorded), InSURE has decreased average throughput. In this case, one can scale out InSURE to meet the data processing demand. Although expending system capacity increases TCO, it is still much economical compared to sending unprocessed data to remote data centers. As shown in Figure 3-22, InSURE brings up to 60% cost savings.

The cost benefit of InSURE increases when local data generation rate increases. Figure 3-23 shows how the total cost of InSURE varies with data generation rate. There is a special point that the cost curve of InSURE interacts with cloud-based data processing. When the data generate rate is below this point (e.g., 0.9 GB/day for our prototype), our system exhibits higher operating cost compared to conventional cloud-based remote processing. If the data rate keeps increasing and researches 0.5 TB per day, our system could yield up to 96% cost reduction due to significantly reduced data transmission overhead.

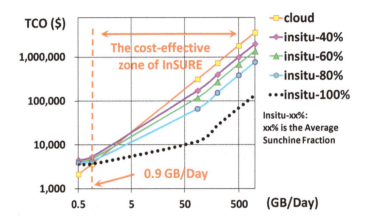

Figure 3-23.   Cost comparison of cloud-based and in-situ computing under different data rate and power budget.

We finally evaluate the cost savings of deploying InSURE in different in-situ big data scenarios. We consider five application scenarios that have different data rates and deployment lengths, as shown in Figure 3-24. For some long-running data acquisition sites, we also consider the hardware replacement cost. Overall, InSURE provides an application-dependent cost saving rate ranging from 15% to 97%.

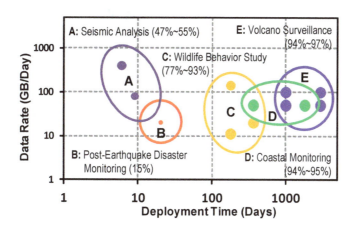

Figure 3-24.   Application-specific cost analysis.

In-situ server clusters are complex systems and many other factors can affect their operating efficiency. For example, the intersection point in Figure 3-23 actually depends on the system capacity. Over-provisioning increases the TCO of InSURE and changes the position of the intersection point. Building efficient, cost-effective in-situ systems requires continued innovation in architecture and system design, which is our future work.

3.7 Key Learning of InSURE

In this study we explore pre-processing of data generated in the field. Specifically, we find that in-situ standalone server system that is powered by renewable energy and backed by green energy buffers is especially promising. We show that efficient energy flow from standalone power supplies to energy buffer and finally to compute nodes is the crux of designing such an in-situ computing facility. This chapter, for the first time, demonstrates the full-system implementation and a novel power management scheme for in-situ standalone server systems. Our system can bring 20~60% performance improvements in terms of system uptime, data throughput, energy availability, and battery lifetime. We believe in-situ systems provide a technically and economically viable

59

way of tackling the incoming data explosion challenge. It will essentially open a door for a

new class of sustainable computing in a world of ubiquitous data.

CHAPTER 4
TOWARDS EFFICIENT SERVER ARCHITECTURE FOR VIRTUALIZED NETWORK FUNCTION DEPLOYMENT: IMPLICATIONS AND IMPLEMENTATIONS

The network is the critical component in the IoT infrastructure. It connects millions of heterogeneous IoT devices and collects vast amount of IoT data, and provides real-time communication between IoT devices and data centers. Intelligence must be distributed across the IoT network based on the application requirements. For example, modern network adopts Mobile-Edge Computing (MEC) and distributing IoT control nodes at the edge for the analysis of latency-sensitive applications.

Network Function Virtualization (NFV) is an initiative driven by the largest service providers (SP) to increase the use of virtualization and integrate intelligence into their network infrastructures. NFV leverages virtualization technology and operates network functions on standard servers to fundamentally decouple the customized and inflexible network hardware. Leading SPs have begun a significant network transformation led by implementations of NFV platforms. NFV and Software-Defined Networking (SDN) provide technology to customize the network to IoT requirements. NFV's ability to distribute computations throughout the network enables near real-time analytics and business intelligence. Today, NFV provides a plethora of virtual network functions (VNFs), including gateways, mobile core, deep packet inspection (DPI), security, routing, and traffic management that can be combined to deliver the customized network services required by IoT.

Recent years have seen a revolution in network infrastructure brought on by the ever-increasing demands for data volume. One promising proposal to emerge from this revolution is Network Functions Virtualization (NFV), which has been widely adopted by service and cloud providers. The essence of NFV is to run network functions as virtualized workloads on commodity Standard High Volume Servers (SHVS), which is the industry standard.

However, our experience using NFV when deployed on modern NUMA-based SHVS paints a frustrating picture. Due to the complexity in the NFV data plane and its service function chain feature, modern NFV deployment on SHVS exhibits a unique processing pattern—heterogeneous software pipeline (HSP), in which the NFV traffic flows must be processed by heterogeneous software components sequentially from the NIC to the end receiver. Since the end-to-end performance of flows is cooperatively determined by the performance of each processing stage, the resource allocation/mapping scheme in NUMA-based SHVS must consider a thread-dependence scheduling to tradeoff the impact of co-located contention and remote packet transmission.

In this paper, we develop a thread scheduling mechanism that collaboratively places threads of HSP to minimize the end-to-end performance slowdown for NFV traffic flow. It employs a dynamic programming-based method to search for the optimal thread mapping with negligible overhead. To serve this mechanism, we also develop a performance slowdown estimation model to accurately estimate the performance slowdown at each stage of HSP. We implement our collaborative thread scheduling mechanism on a real system and evaluate it using real workloads. On average, our algorithm outperforms state-of-the-art NUMA-aware and contention-aware scheduling policies by at least 7% on CPU utilization and 23% on traffic throughput with negligible computational overhead (less than 1 second).

4.1 NUMA Challenges NFV Performance

Today's service providers need greater performance, flexibility, and adaptability from the network services that support them. Gartner forecasts that the number of devices connected to the Internet of Things (IoT) will reach 26 billion by 2020, and impose an unprecedented challenge to data transmission services and data center network infrastructures. To meet the rapidly increasing volume of traffic and deliver both capital (Capex) and operational (Opex) expenditure advantages, thirteen of the world's largest service providers (AT&T, Verizon, China Mobile, CenturyLink, etc.) propose Network Functions Virtualization (NFV) [2] . NFV allows data center networking functions such as load balancing, firewalls, and switching to be implemented as software or virtual machine-based Virtualized Network Functions (VNF). The VNFs are consolidated on cost-effective Standard High Volume Servers (SHVS) with software switching instead of fixed-function specialized hardware. By doing so, NFV creates highly flexible and adaptable network resources that can be deployed quickly to respond to changing demands at lower cost. To date, NFV has gained over 220 industry participants including the Linux Foundation OPNFV [61]. According to a recent study, the global NFV market is expected to grow 52% from 2013-2018.

Because SHVS are expected to continue to serve as the backbone for all network infrastructure, their performance when running VNFs must be considered. Intel has proposed an initial x86-based reference server architecture, Intel Open Network Platform [62], to enable NFV deployment. However, we observe current SHVS architecture support for NFV deployment falls short on generality and flexibility, and is not fully prepared for NFV. For example, although existing hardware-based high performance I/O technologies such as Single Root I/O Virtualization (SR-IOV) [63] and Data Direct I/O

(DDIO) [64] can achieve line rate VM-to-network throughput by bypassing the hypervisor layer, they do not support overlay-based network virtualization for multi-tenant and VM migration, making them less flexible in modern SDN/NFV deployment. More importantly, VM-to-VM traffic, which is dominant in NFV enabled environments, must traverse the PCI Express bus in SR-IOV and DDIO, leading to throughput that is inferior to the throughput in a software switch.

In this study, we characterize the architectural overhead of SHVS using real Telco and cloud NFV workloads. We observe that NFV deployment presents more performance demanding and complex processing patterns than typical IT workloads. In a NFV environment, a packet flow needs to traverse the end-to-end data path, namely the NFV data plane, which includes a variety of software components that reside within VNFs (e.g. virtual NICs and packet processing routines within VNFs) and hypervisor virtualization stacks (e.g. physical NICs, hypervisor I/O handler, virtual switch threads). A VNF may also process traffic flows in tandem with other VNFs in service chains. We term this packet processing style as a Heterogeneous Software Pipeline (HSP).

The software pipeline is a parallel application that consists of several communicating stages that process streams of input data in tandem. This processing style demands end-to-end performance guarantees (either throughput or latency) for network flows. This indicates that the performance of an HSP is cooperatively determined by the performance of each processing stage throughout the processing path. In other words, the end-to-end performance slowdown of an NFV flow is the aggregated slowdown at each pipeline stage.

Since all software components in the pipeline are deployed on the shared computing resources of SHVS, finding efficient and effective resource allocation/mapping schemes for these software components, or threads, is of the utmost importance. However, existing SHVS hardware resource allocation schemes and performance estimation models lack support for software pipeline-style applications. Specifically, when a packet is passed between software components or threads that belong to neighboring pipeline stages, the performance slowdown for this packet at this stage can be decomposed into the slowdown caused by resource interference and the slowdown caused by inter-thread communication.

Though current thread and core allocation methods [65] can manage the former slowdown, they overlook the performance slowdown caused by inter-stage data transfer overheads. Considering that Non-Uniform Memory Access (NUMA) [27] architectures are ubiquitously adopted in contemporary SHVS, the message pass/packet transfer between stages in HSP causes the thread to access data from the memory of its predecessor thread, while its predecessor's memory may reside in remote NUMA nodes. Therefore, the inter-thread communication overheads must be factored in the performance slowdown estimation model in accordance with interference based model to provide thread-dependence scheduling in each stage of the software pipeline.

Designing the aggregated performance slowdown estimation model for end-to-end data path in NFV raises several questions. How can one quantify the performance slowdown caused by interference and communication at each stage? Moreover, how can these be combined into a comprehensive slowdown model? Finally, how can one compare the performance slowdown in the presence of varying resource sensitivities at each stage? To address these issues, we present a new performance model for estimating the end-to-end performance slowdown of flows in software pipeline processing environments such as NFV. Our model assesses the intra-stage performance slowdown caused by hardware resource contention and inter-thread/core communication overheads. It also estimates the end-to-end performance slowdown by summing the weighted inter-stage slowdown at each stage.

Leveraging our holistic performance estimation model, we design vFlowComb, a dynamic thread mapping mechanism that enables thread-dependence mapping for NFV service chains. To achieve this goal, vFlowComb features a Collaborative Thread Scheduling (CTS) mechanism that guarantees to minimize the end-to-end performance slowdown for each NIC hardware queue. CTS exploits a novel Dynamic Programming-Based Mechanism (DPBM) to find the thread-core mapping with the minimum aggregate performance slowdown, while considerably reducing the performance sampling and decision-making overheads.

This paper makes the following contributions:

- We explore the deployment of modern NFV workloads on current SHVS architectures. We observe that NFV adopts a heterogeneous software pipeline (HSP) processing style, which presents significant challenges for current thread mapping mechanisms and performance estimation tools.

- We explore the performance slowdown in the HSP on modern NUMA based architectures. We propose a performance estimation model that evaluates the performance slowdown of each stage of HSP by synergistically considering hardware resource contention and inter-thread/core communication overheads.

66

- Based on our performance slowdown estimation model, we propose vFlowComb; a thread mapping mechanism that minimizes the end-to-end performance slowdown. We implement vFlowComb using Open vSwitch and OpenStack.

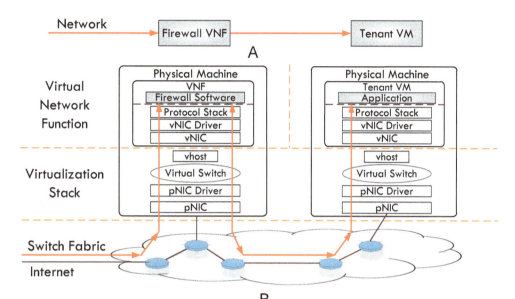

Figure 4-1.   Heterogeneous software pipeline (HSP) in NFV data plane.

4.2 Background and Motivation

4.2.1 Network Functions Virtualization

(1) Control/Data Plane

In software-defined networks, the network environment can be split into three planes: the application plane, the control plane, and the data plane. Tenants interact with the application plane, requesting deployment of their virtual private networks. The control plane responds to these requests and instantiates virtual links between tenant VMs and VNFs using tunneling techniques or encapsulation policies. The data plane instantiates configurations furnished by the control plane and provides a network traffic backbone for each tenant's virtual private network. The data plane consists of all tenant VMs and VNFs, and the virtual switches by which they are connected. All components are consolidated on an SHVS architecture and are allocated on shared computing resources.

Figure 4-1A shows a simple tenant virtual network with a VM and a firewall. In this setup, all incoming traffic must pass through a firewall before entering the tenant VM. Each packet will traverse the software components before being processed in the VNF and the VM.

(2) Software Pipeline in Data Plane

Here, we describe the detailed processing patterns of the software pipeline in NFV data plane and illustrate a software pipeline implementation based on the Linux kernel with NAPI, a virtual machine, and an Open vSwitch-based software switch. Each software component receives packets from its predecessor, processes them based on its functionality, and sends them to the successor components, as shown in Figure 4-1B.

When an incoming packet arrives at the input buffer of a physical NIC, it will be DMA'ed to the kernel DMA RX-buffer, sk_buff, which is allocated in main memory. In multi-10G networks, this buffer allocation/de-allocation could significantly stress the memory subsystem (tens of millions of allocations per second). Once in the buffer, a hardware interrupt is triggered. An interrupt handler associated with one of the processor cores is called and schedules a softIRQ context to its local core or another CPU core. All CPU cores examine their poll queue using the poll method and process the queued softIRQ context. Modern NICs support multiple receive and transmit descriptor queues (multi-queue) technique. The NIC controller computes a hash value for each incoming packet. Based on these hash values, the NIC assigns packets of the same data flow to a single queue and distributes traffic flows evenly across queues. To maximize the network transmission performance in multi-core server systems, Receive-side Scaling (RSS) and Receive Packet Steering (RPS) are used. RSS enables multiple NIC queues to have their own associated CPU core while RPS assigns a specific core for a softIRQ context. These core assignments should be carefully designed to avoid unbalanced CPU loads.

(3) Virtual Switch

In virtual machines, the hypervisor provides intra-server networking connectivity for virtual machines. In this virtual network, the hypervisor creates one or more virtual NICs (vNICs) for each VM to connect to physical NICs (pNICs) of the host server and facilitates network connection between the VM network stack and hypervisor network stack through virtualized switches (e.g. Linux Net bridge and Open vSwitch) [66].

When using virtual switches, the intra-server network connection is no longer limited by network speed but memory bandwidth since no packet must pass through PCI-E links to special purpose hardware. This enables high-performance communication among VMs. More importantly, virtual switches enable cross-server bridging in a way that makes the underlying server architecture transparent. A virtual switch within one server can transparently join with another virtual switch in another server, simplifying VM migration.

4.2.2 NFV Workloads

In this paper, we use Clearwater [67] as our NFV platform. Clearwater is a cloud-based Telco-grade IP Multimedia Subsystem (IMS). IMS is widely adopted by large Telcos to provide IP-based voice, video, and messaging services based on soft-switching. Clearwater consists of a series of typical function components with various resource utilization patterns in a Telco data center, and could be easily deployed as VNFs in NFV environment.

(1) Workloads Description

Bono is a scalable edge proxy in the NFV environment. It serves as a gateway and provides connections to the Clearwater system for clients. Sprout processes the incoming requests from Bono, acting as a registrar and authoritative routing proxy. The Sprout cluster includes a memcached cluster to store client registration data. Homestead provides web services interface to Sprout for retrieving authentication credentials and user profile information; providing a subscriber server and employs Cassandra as the backing store for its managed data.

(2) Testing Methodology for Clearwater

We deploy Clearwater as virtual machines in our characterization and evaluation. In this chapter, we use SIPp [68] to generate real world Telco NFV traffic. It is a performance-testing tool for Telco infrastructure and can establish and release multiple calls to an NFV cluster. We choose user registration and deregistration (reg-dereg) calls for the traffic flow in this paper. A reg-dereg call consists of three requests: one for registration, one for authentication, and one for deregistration. SIPp initiates each call with an initiated call rate. If a response to a request times out (10s), the call will be tagged as failed. SIPp initiates call with an initiated call rate. Each round of experiment runs for 300s. We run 5 trials and take the average results. We use the Successful Call Rate (SCR), which is used as an indicator of the service quality of the NFV system. SCR gives the ratio of the successful call rate to the initiated call rate. The maximum SCR is 1.

4.2.3 Network I/O NUMA

With NUMA architectures, each socket (i.e. processor node) is associated with a local memory node through the memory controller. Multiple cores in one socket share the last level cache, memory controller, and PCI-e interface (e.g. NIC) through the

intra-socket interconnect. Inter-socket communications are enabled through

point-to-point high-speed interconnects (e.g. Intel's QPI). In a multi-socket server with

NUMA enabled, the PCI devices are associated with a subgroup of NUMA nodes, as

shown in Figure 4-2.

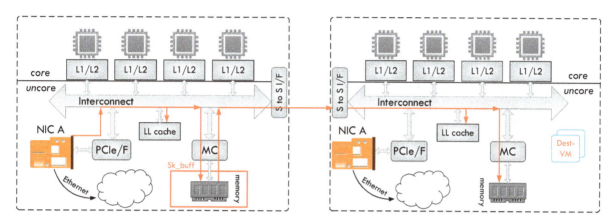

Figure 4-2.   I/O NUMA.

4.3 Characterizing NFV Workloads in SHVS

We characterize the performance of NFV flow to identify inefficiencies in current

NUMA-based SHVS from the viewpoint of architecture level.

4.3.1 Characterization Setup

(1) Hardware Platform

Our physical platform configuration is shown in Table 4-1. The system uses four

Intel X520 SPF+ 10 Gigabit Ethernet NICs divided into two groups and are associated

with two NUMA nodes respectively. To clearly expose the bottlenecks, we configured the

IBM x3850 system as 2 sockets and only use one NIC in the characterization.

(2) Software Platform

We use the open source cloud platform OpenStack Kilo [69] to build a full-fledged

cloud environment for NFV deployment. Our test cloud consists of three compute nodes, one cloud controller node, and one networking node. All compute nodes run RHEL 6.4.

The network service Neutron helps tenants to build their own private software defined

networks and Open vSwitch based virtual switches. All VNFs and tenant VMs are

deployed as virtual machines with 2 vCPU and 4GB memory. The VMs are consolidated

on NUMA-based SHVS. They communicate with each other using GRE [70]. The

networking hierarchy is shown in Figure 4-3.

Table 4-1.　Hardware platform configurations

Item	Value
SHVS system	IBM x3850 X5, 8-socket NUMA
Processor	Intel Xeon X7550, 2.0GHz (Nehalem) 8 physical cores (16 with Hyper-Threading)/socket 18MB L3 cache for each socket 64KB L1 cache and 256KB L2 cache for each core
Memory	64GB, DDR3 for each socket, 512GB in total
Interconnection	Intel QuickPath Interconnect, 6.4GT/s
NIC	Intel X520 10GB, Mellanox 40GB Associate with socket 0 and 4

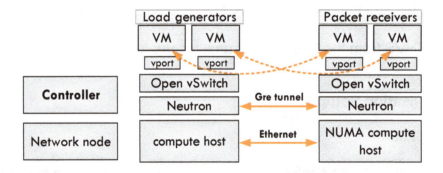

Figure 4-3.　Framework setup.

(3) Workloads

Our real world NFV workloads are introduced in 4.2. To clearly identify the

bottlenecks, we also use the network intensive micro-benchmark Netperf [71] to

generate UDP STREAM and TCP STREAM as stable and controllable traffic loads. As

shown in Figure 4-3, we deploy NFV workloads or simple networking workloads on

VNFs/tenant VMs as packet receivers. We deploy client VMs on other machines as load generators.

4.3.2 Characterization of Heterogeneous Software Pipeline on NUMA based SHVS

We investigate the performance and architectural behaviors of current NUMA-based SHVS when executing heterogeneous software component pipeline in NFV deployment. We vary the thread-to-socket/core mapping and co-located contention applications to examine the performance trade-offs in HSP. These results indicate that new performance modeling tools are needed.

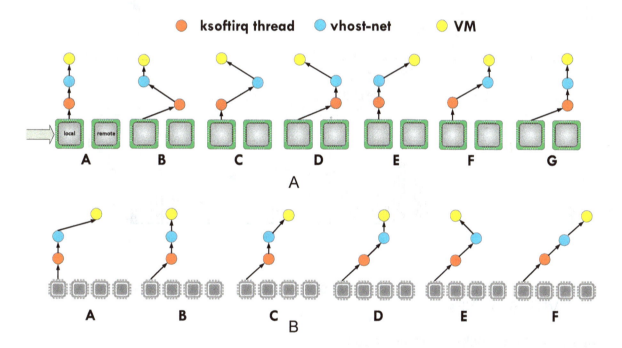

Figure 4-4.   Thread mapping configurations, A) Thread-to-socket configurations. B) Thread-to-core configurations (threads are mapped on the same socket).

(1) Methodology

As we described in 4.2, the flow path in the NFV data plane can be seen as a packet traversing the software components. The software components in the NFV data plane are the ksoftirq kernel thread that handles the NAPI routine and the virtual switch

73

routing process in which the packets are written to TAP's socket buffer, and the vhost-net thread that copies the packets from the socket buffer to the VM's vNIC buffer. In this characterization, we focus on the packet receiving process (i.e. incoming flow processing) since it contains all of the critical software components in the NFV data plane. We collect the architectural statistics using Intel's Performance Counter Monitor tools [72].

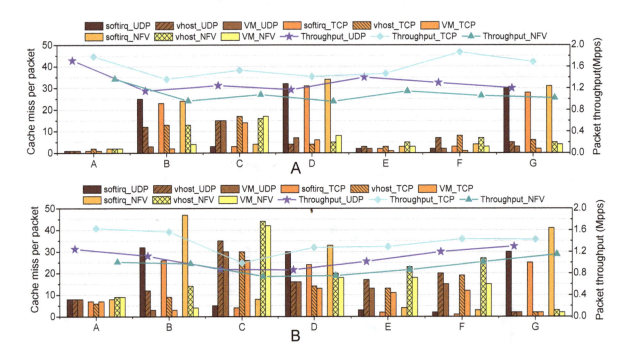

Figure 4-5.   Performance and architectural behaviors of Inter-socket scenarios, A) 1 VNF. B) 5 VNFs.

(2) Impacts of Inter-socket Communications

We first vary the thread-to-socket mappings to investigate the impact of inter-socket communication (CPU-to-CPU and CPU-to-RAM) on the performance of HSP. In this experiment, we study seven different thread-to-socket mappings with different socket affinities for the ksoftirq kernel thread, the vhost-net thread, and the VM thread. The different configurations, A-G, are shown in Figure 4-4A. A local node

74

consists of a NUMA node and a NIC. Different threads on the same socket are mapped onto different cores. We consider three network traffic loads. We use Netperf to generate 1400B UDP packets and 64KB TCP packets. We also use SIPp to generate a traffic flow at a rate of 300 calls/second. We report the cache miss per packet and received packet throughput (packet per second) in Figure 4-5A. For the NFV loads, we report the successful call rate as defined in 4.2.

For the UDP flow we can observe approximately 30 LLC misses per packet in the ksoftirq in configuration G. This is caused by the inter-socket DMA transmission overhead since the incoming packets should be brought into LLC for ksoftirq processing on the remote NUMA node. In configuration E, we can observe there are around 5 LLC misses per packet in the vhost-net and VM threads, and nearly no LLC misses at ksoftirq. This is because vhost-net needs to access the vNIC of the target VM across the sockets. We can also observe the traffic throughput increases from 1.2Mpps to 1.45Mpps, while the collocated ksoftirq, vhost-net, and VM gain the highest throughput at 1.71Mpps.

To examine a real NFV deployment scenario, we increase the VM consolidation (5 VMs) and traffic flow and re-run the tests. We present the results in Figure 4-5B. We can observe the performance in configuration E experiences a severe drop. The LLC misses per packet for the VM and vhost-net threads increase to around 20 misses per packet and the traffic throughput drops from 1.4Mpps to 1.02Mpps. This is because intensive inter-socket communication occurs between the vhost-net thread and the vNIC buffers.

Finding 1: In this experiment, we observe that the inter-socket communication overheads caused by asymmetry in NUMA-based SHVS significantly impact the performance of heterogeneous software pipeline workloads like NFV.

Finding 2: The thread heterogeneity of each stage in a software pipeline exhibits sensitivity to hardware resources and inter-socket communication overheads, while also being related to workload intensity. For example, we can observe the inter-thread communication between ksoftirq and vhost-net is more sensitive to inter-socket access than inter-thread communication between the NIC driver and ksoftirq when more VMs are consolidated.

Finding 3. The thread heterogeneity of each stage incurs heterogeneous performance slowdown at each stage. However, the low-performance slowdown at an earlier stage does not necessarily result in a low end-to-end performance slowdown for the whole pipeline. In Figure 4-5B, it is clear that configuration E exhibits lower slowdown at the NIC-ksoftirq stage than configuration G does, even though its end-to-end throughput is lower than G.

(3) Impacts of Intra-socket Co-located Contention

We further investigate the performance of a heterogeneous software pipeline in the presence of intra-socket co-located contention. We study the performance slowdown caused by the contention of co-located software components and other user workloads to derive the performance implications.

We first investigate the impact of thread-to-core mappings. We design six thread-to-core mappings as shown in Figure 4-4B. In each mapping, all threads (ksoftirq kernel thread, vhost-net thread, and VM thread) are mapped onto the same NUMA

76

socket and may use SMT sharing. We repeat the procedure from 4.3.2, using 4VMs in this case due to the limits of available cores, and report the cache miss per packet and traffic throughput in Figure 4-6.

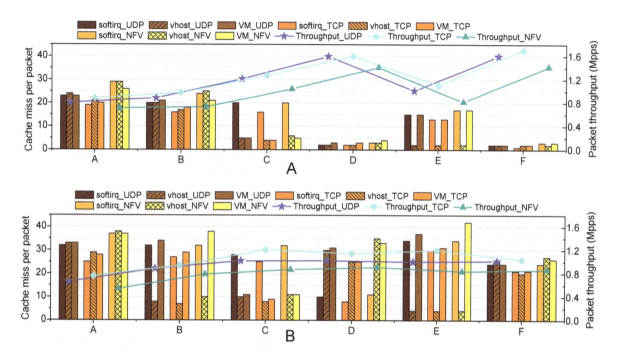

Figure 4-6.   Performance and architectural behaviors of Intra-socket scenarios, A) 1 VNF. B) 4 VNFs.

We observe that the throughput in configurations A, B and E is significantly lower to the other configurations in the single VM scenario. In addition, the LLC misses per packet at ksoftirq and VM are very high (around 35 misses per packet). This is because the VM is running in user space while the ksoftirq is running in kernel space. The frequent context switching leads to severe performance degradation.

Finding 4: The ksoftirq and VM threads are very contentious. It would be better to co-locate them on separate CMP cores, not on single core with SMT.

77

Finding 5: All scenarios will come across performance bottlenecks when more VMs are consolidated. Intensive resource sharing causes very high cache misses at all threads, limiting throughput due to resource contention.

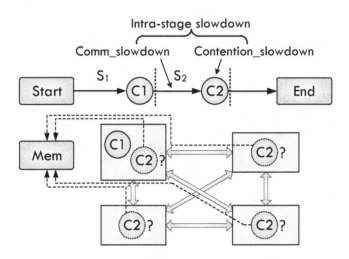

Figure 4-7.   Intra-stage performance slowdown.

4.3.3 Performance Slowdown Model

Motivated by our characterizations of the HSP inter-socket communication overheads and intra-socket co-located contention overheads, we observe the necessity to find the best trade-off between them. Though many prior studies have explored application slowdown caused by resource sharing or asymmetric communication overheads [41, 46, 73-76], they are designed for evaluating the overall slowdown for applications. There is not an explicit model to measure the inter-stage performance slowdown that coordinately considers both the communication overhead and application slowdown at each thread core in HSP. We develop an enhanced estimation model to solve this problem.

We partition an HSP into several stages; each stage consists of a thread and its communication path. The intra-stage performance slowdown is caused by the inter-socket communication overhead (potential) and application contention slowdown at current stage thread, as depicted in Figure 4-7.

We build our estimation model based on mature NUMA-aware performance analysis models [26, 27] and our empirical studies. When a thread accesses remote memory (e.g. C2 accesses memory of C1), the performance degradation is caused by four factors: memory controller contention (MC), interconnect contention (IC), last-level cache (LC) and remote access latency (RL). To estimate the inter-stage overheads caused by inter-socket access, we explore how these factors contribute to the HSP inter-stage performance degradation. We conduct a series of experiments where the socket affinities of ksoftirq, vhost-net, and VM threads (configurations E, F, and G in 4.3.2) are gradually altered. We then vary the contention flow number for each. We present the overheads contribution factors for all three stages, as shown in Figure 4-8.

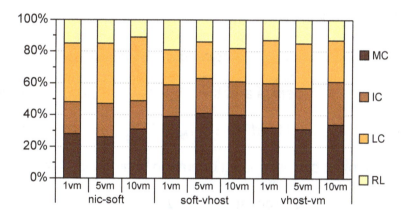

Figure 4-8.   Architectural overheads contribution factors.

We can observe that, though the four factors' contributions to performance degradation change slightly when input flow numbers vary, different stages still manifest typical distributions. For example, the ksoftirq is more sensitive to LC and vhost-net is more sensitive to MC, which can be expected based on the characterizations in 4.3.2.

Liu [27] proposes to use Performance Monitoring Units (PMU) to quantify the four factors. In this solution, the reciprocal of last level cache hit rate (L3_hit) is used for evaluating the LC. The cycle loss due to L3 misses (cycle_loss) is used to evaluate the MC. The cycle_loss at the remote node is used to measure IC. The RL is expressed by the ratio between local IPC to remote IPC. The correlation coefficients between some PMU readings and the corresponding NUMA overheads are around 0.9. However, [27] estimates the NUMA overheads by naively adding up all four PMU readings. This may lead to less accurate evaluation results since different NUMA performance factors have various contributions to the inter-socket NUMA overhead at a stage. This is unacceptable in HSP, because the accumulated error estimation at each stage may lead to large deviations.

We present an enhanced model that estimates the intra-stage overheads as a weighted sum of PMU readings. Take the intra-stage overheads calculation between C1 and C2 for example. There are four socket candidates for thread C2. For each socket candidate, the required PMU metrics are: the $L3\_hit|_{candidate\_socket}$, the $cycle\_loss|_{C1\_socket}$, the $cycle\_loss|_{candidate\_socket}$, and the $IPC|_{C1\_socket} / IPC|_{candidate\_socket}$. The required PMU metrics are weighted to the corresponding overhead contribution factor at this stage. The weighted sum indicates the inter-socket overhead between the C1 socket and the candidate sockets at this stage. We call this sum the performance slowdown index.

Now we possess a performance estimation model that is capable of evaluating the performance slowdown of a stage of HSP. We validate this model by examining the end-to-end performance slowdown in a series of experiments. In the validation, we test three scenarios, configurations E, F, and G as shown in Figure 4-4A, since they are the typical scenarios with inter-socket communication at different stages in an HSP. We vary the input flow number and present the corresponding performance slowdown index, as shown in Figure 4-9. The results illustrate that our revised architectural metrics can accurately identify performance differences among different stages in HSP. Given that, we can use it as an indicator for our thread scheduling scheme that is tailored to HSP.

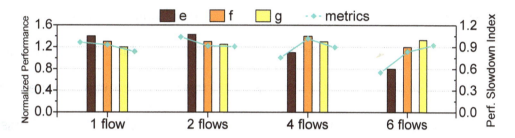

Figure 4-9.　Validation of performance slowdown index.

4.4 vFlowComb: Efficient Thread Scheduling for NFV Deployment

We present vFlowComb, an architecture support thread mapping framework based on our HSP overheads estimation model. vFlowComb facilitates traffic load-aware and priority-aware data plane hardware resource scheduling and provides a guarantee on the end-to-end NFV flow performance on SHVS architecture. We introduce vFlowComb based on the Open vSwitch implementation. To achieve this goal, vFlowComb exploits a Collaborative Thread Mapping Scheme (CTM). It features a dynamic programming-based thread-mapping scheme (DPBM) to coordinate thread scheduling in the NFV service chain.

4.4.1 Preliminary

Flexible and accurate NFV delivery requires that more data, such as core affinity of VNFs, flow throughput, and NIC hardware queue-flow mappings, be exposed to the NFV data plane. Current NICs equipped with hardware-based packet classification support this capability. Although beyond the scope of this paper, we can also implement software-/hardware-based packet classification schemes for specific protocols to improve flexibility and reduce CapEx. In this study we assume that we can obtain NIC hardware queue-flow mapping, thread affinities and target VNF information for incoming flows, flow priorities, and throughputs.

4.4.2 Collaborative Threads Scheduling

Contrasted to conventional thread scheduling mechanisms that only focus on thread co-location contention mitigation [77], we present a Collaborative Threads Scheduling (CTS) mechanism that guarantees end-to-end performance in the HSP. Specifically, we extend the existing contention-aware thread scheduling mechanism by establishing a new dimension that also considers inter-thread communication overhead between predecessor and successor threads in a service chain.

We begin by introducing the system models. All software components in an application constitute a software pipeline (e.g. NFV service chains and virtual switch threads). Each service chain, k, forms a pipeline, P_k, with N_k stages. All service chains share the same source node, s, but terminate on a different node, v_d. Every stage, S_j, is characterized by its communication overhead, o_j, with the predecessor stage, S_{j-1}. For example, packets belonging to network flow F_k will be handled by pipeline P_k and will be processed by a corresponding thread at each stage. This thread will be mapped to core v_m.

The problem can be defined as: given a set of K weighted flows, $F = \{F_1, F_2, ..., F_K\}$, with weights, $W = \{w_1, w_2, ..., w_K\}$, where the weights express priority levels and each flow has fixed source and destination nodes, optimize the overall weighted system throughput/latency by finding the optimal thread-core mapping for the individual flows.

The problem is analogous to a single source shortest path problem where the communication overheads are used as distances.

To find the optimal thread-core mapping, the thread scheduler must consider all possible thread-socket/core mapping combinations for a given flow. However, an exhaustive search would result in exponential complexity, $O(c^n)$, which cannot meet the requirement of adaptive mappings at runtime. We propose an algorithm based on dynamic programming (DP) that derives optimal solutions for minimizing the end-to-end performance slowdown using M cores to execute flow F_k. We define a recursive function, $\delta_j(s, v_m)$, for each core candidate, v_m, in stage S_j to store the thread-core mapping configuration that achieves the minimized aggregated slowdown at stage S_j, where $o(u, v)$ is the performance slowdown between u and v. Giving:

$$\delta_j(s, v) = \min\{\delta(s, u) + o(u, v) \mid u \notin S_j, v \in S_j \} \tag{4-1}$$

Let $F_{k,j}$ be a sub-flow of flow F_k that only includes stages S_1 to S_j of F_k. The goal is to find the optimal thread-core mapping that achieves the minimized aggregated slowdown for flow $F_{k,j}$. In this scenario, the aggregated slowdown indicated by $\delta_j(s, v_m)$ at stage S_j only depends on the aggregated slowdown indicated by $\delta_j(s, v_l)$ at previous stage S_{j-1} and the intra-stage performance slowdown index, $o(v_l, v_m)$, between v_m and v_l. we can rewrite the function as:

$$\delta_j(s, v_m) = \min\{\delta_{j-1}(s, v_l) + o(v_l, v_m) \mid v_m \in S_j, v_l \in S_{j-1} \} \tag{4-2}$$

The dynamic programming starts by computing the aggregated slowdown at each core in stage S_1. The DP continues to compute the aggregated slowdown at each core in stage S_2. Since the programming already stored the minimized aggregated slowdown path from the source node to the cores at the first stage, the minimized aggregated slowdown at a core in stage S_2 can be easily calculated by choosing the minimal sum of

the aggregated slowdown at a given core in stage S_1 and the slowdown index between

the stage S_2 core and stage S_1 core. Thus, iteratively, an optimal solution is achieved

because all combinations of thread-core mappings are considered. However, the

complexity is reduced since optimal solutions are stored in tables and do not need to be

recomputed. Since vFlowComb schedules thread mappings based on NIC queue, the

space/time complexity is $O(MN_k)$ for mapping one NIC hardware queue.

Table 4-2.   DPBM algorithm

Algorithm 1. Aggregated Slowdown Minimization
Input: K weighted flows F with N_k stages, M_j cores in stage S_j, the aggregated slowdown $o(v_l, v_m)$ at core v_m,
Output: The thread-core mapping table R that achieves the minimized aggregated slowdown for the flow F.
  1: Initialize R, $\delta(s, v)$
  2: for j=1 to N_k do
  3:   for $v_m \in S_j$ do
  4:     **if** j=1 **then**
  5:       $\delta_1(s, v_m) = o(v_m, s)$
  6:     **else**
  7:       $\delta_j(s, v_m) = \min\{\delta_{j-1}(s, v_l) + o(v_l, v_m) \mid v_l \in S_{j-1}\}$
  8:     **endif**
  9:     R.append(v_m)
10:   end
11: return R

We incorporate the CTS mechanism into vFlowComb to handle thread-chain

scheduling in a real NFV environment. Figure 4-10 illustrates a typical workflow of CTS

in vFlowComb. We assume we can obtain the NIC queue-flow mapping and destination

VNFs for each flow by leveraging current NIC hardware. Based on this initial mapping

information, CTS aims to efficiently map the software components (ksoftirq and vhost-net

threads) in NFV HSP to improve the performance of NFV flows and resource utilization

of SHVS.

84

The typical workflow of vFlowComb is as follows.

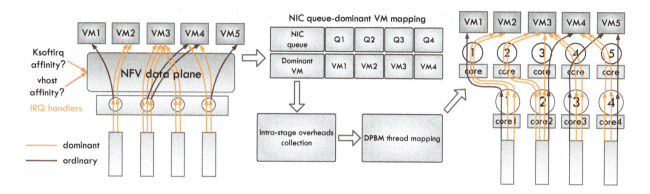

Figure 4-10.   An overview of vFlowComb workflow.

Dominant VNF identification: In this stage, vFlowComb analyzes a snapshot of system flow patterns to identify the priority VNFs and critical flows. To achieve practical efficiency, vFlowComb schedules threads for dominant flows of each NIC queue instead of for a single flow. vFlowComb oversees the flow distribution at each NIC queue and identifies a target VNF with the highest incoming flow traffic (aggregated packets per second) from this NIC queue. vFlowComb then defines this VNF as the dominant target VNF for this NIC queue and schedules a thread chain between them. If vFlowComb detects a dominant VNF is a priority VNF, the corresponding NIC queue will be tagged as a priority queue. Finally, vFlowComb obtains a queue group, $\{Q_1, Q_2, Q_3..., Q_m\}$, which is sorted by priority and flow traffic.

Core pool allocation: vFlowComb collects the available core information and divides the cores into different groups; cores will either be in the ksoftirq core group, $\{kC_1, kC_2, kC_3,..., kC_n\}$, or in the vhost-net core group, $\{vC_1, vC_2, vC_3,..., vC_n\}$. The benefits of a differentiated core pool are twofold. First, it helps the DP by greatly reducing the search space, which increases the efficiency of CTS. Second, since cores in certain stage only need to sample intra-stage overheads to the cores/sockets in the next stage, it reduces

85

the amount of data collection in the performance slowdown model. When allocating a core to the core pool, vFlowComb prefers the core with the lowest utilization. This provides more performance headroom for threads in early stages so that the global $\delta(s, v_m)$ for each core will not be refreshed frequently.

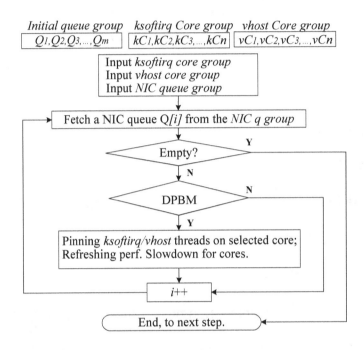

Figure 4-11.   Flowchart of DPBM.

Intra-stage performance slowdown collection: Obtaining intra-stage performance slowdown statistics is critical for implementing CTS. During the data collection period, each core in a stage (e.g. C1) traverses the core pool of the next stage (e.g. C2) and queries the PMU readings. The data that is returned will be preserved in a table that is maintained by the core. In fact, for each PMU query, all returned PMU readings are socket-based, which reduces the number of inter-processor interrupts between queryer and queryee. From this, the intra-stage performance slowdown between cores in neighboring pools can be established.

Threads scheduling: We apply dynamic programming based mapping (DPBM) to CTS to conduct thread-core scheduling. As shown in Figure 4-11, CTS assigns the ksoftirq core and vhost-net core using DPBM for each queue in the sequence. vFlowComb maintains the global $\delta(s, v_m)$ for each core, v_m. After a queue is mapped, the intra-stage performance slowdown and $\delta(s, v_m)$ of all impacted cores will be refreshed to avoid inaccurate scheduling for the next queue.

Our implementation is based on Receive Packet Steering (RPS) feature provided by the Linux kernel. First, RPS selects CPU cores to execute SoftIRQ based on hash values (skb->rxhash) calculated from received packet headers. Next, the rps_get_cpu function selects a SoftIRQ core based on the sock_flow_table that contains hash/core relation pairs. Finally, the enqueue_to_backlog function executes SoftIRQ on the core.

4.5 Evaluation

vFlowComb provides end-to-end performance guarantees for NFV workloads by cooperatively scheduling the critical threads in the heterogeneous software pipeline. We evaluate the effectiveness of leveraging vFlowComb to improve the performance of heterogeneous software pipeline on current NUMA-based SHVS platform. We also discuss the design space in vFlowComb.

4.5.1 Effectiveness of Collaborative Threads Scheduling

We evaluate the effectiveness of CTS using various traffic loads and co-located contention intensities.

(1) Methodology

NFV environment: The test scenarios are designed to mimic real service chains in NFV deployment, as shown in Figure 4-12. Each service chain consists of no more than 3 VNFs. Each VNF uses 2 vCPU with 4GB memory. All VNFs are deployed on NUMA machine.

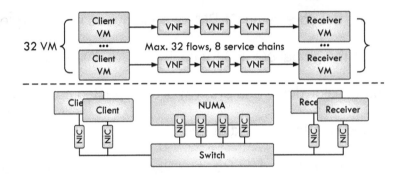

Figure 4-12.   NFV environment setup for evaluation.

We set up 4 dedicated servers (2 clients and 2 receivers). Each server is connected to a 10GB NIC. We deploy 32 VMs on the clients and receivers as traffic generators and traffic sinks, respectively. They can generate a maximum of 32 traffic flows, which can be processed by 8 service chains. The traffic flows are processed by VNFs in the service chain in tandem through the virtual switches.

NFV workloads: We evaluate vFlowComb using TCP traffic and Telco NFV traffic. For TCP traffic, we set all VNFs as packet forwarding components. For real NFV traffic, the VNFs are deployed as Clearwater components, as described in 4.2. We generate heavy and medium traffic by tuning the packet generation rate (packet per second) at the generators. At each client VM, we use Netperf to generate 512B TCP_STREAM traffic at 24Kpps (medium) and 32Kpps (heavy). We use a small packet size to maximize the system stress. For the NFV workload reg-dereg, we set the input call rate as 300 call/s (medium) and 500 call/s (heavy) and for reg-invite, we set the input call rate as 100 call/s (medium) and 150 calls/s (heavy). The gateway of the NFV deployment employs a load balancer so that the traffic flows are balanced among service chains based on VNF loads.

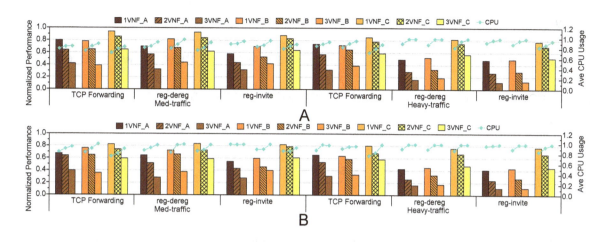

Figure 4-13. Average end-to-end traffic flow performance and average system CPU utilization, A) No contention. B) With contention.

Test cases: We test all three traffic loads (TCP STREAM, reg-dereg, and reg-invite) using input traffic capacity, VNF number in the service chain, and co-located contention. First, we vary the input traffic capacity. Second, we vary the different VNF numbers in a service chain. For TCP traffic, we change the length of the service chain by adding or reducing the number of packet forwarding VMs. For the Telco traffics, we change the VNF number by consolidating the Clearwater function modules on the remaining VNFs. Finally, we vary the co-located contention on the NUMA machine. In the contention scenario we co-locate eight VMs running a single instance of GraphAnalytic from CloudSuite [56]. Each test case lasts 300s. We report the average end-to-end traffic flow performance and average system CPU utilization in Figure 4-13. Note that we report the normalized performance of different traffic loads. For TCP traffic, we report the packet receive rate, which is the ratio of received packets to the sent packets, with a maximum value of 1. For the Telco traffics, we report the successful call rate as defined in 4.2.2.

Baseline scheduling polices: We use two baseline scheduling policies. The first policy is a NUMA node-aware scheduling policy (A). This policy schedules all threads in the flow data path onto the destination VNF socket. The second policy is a contention-aware scheduling policy (B). It places threads on the core with the least performance slowdown, but ignores the inter-socket communication overheads.

(2) Overall Performance Improvement Analysis

From Figure 4-13 we can draw several key insights that show the benefits of vFlowComb.

Overall benefits: In all scenarios, we observe that vFlowComb outperforms other methods in terms of average end-to-end performance and global CPU usage. Though the end-to-end performance improvement may be not significantly improved in some scenarios, we can always expect at least 7% global CPU usage savings brought by vFlowComb.

Benefits for the long service chain: When there are 3 VNFs in the service chain, both A and B suffer significant performance degradation. The contention-aware policy performs slightly better than NUMA-aware policy since global contention increases with the more consolidated VNFs. Nevertheless, vFlowComb is still able to avoid performance degradation by finding the best flow data path with the least end-to-end performance slowdown, while saving global CPU resources.

Benefits for the latency sensitive traffic loads: The successful call rate is determined by the request response time. Both reg-dereg and reg-invite are TCP traffics with mixed packet sizes. In medium traffic scenarios, vFlowComb demonstrates about 20% more successful call rate than A and B. When the input call rate is increased, vFlowComb can average 50% more successful calls than A and B. Compared to stable stream traffic, vFlowComb performs a little worse when running Telco workloads (about

90

14% performance degradation). This is because the packet size and flow direction vary frequently in Telco traffic, while vFlowComb works under a low PMU sampling rate (1 sample/s) to reduce the computation overheads. Nevertheless, vFlowComb still outperforms the baseline policies with performance improvements from 15% to 100%.

(3) Zoomed Performance Improvement Analysis

We further examine the effectiveness of vFlowComb when processing extremely high throughput traffic flows. In this test, we zoom in the packet receiving process. We employ a client machine and a receiver machine to establish a peer-to-peer network. We opt to use the Mellanox 40 GB NICs to completely remove any NIC bottleneck. We deploy various numbers of VMs (8, 16, 24, and 32) on the client machine and deploy the corresponding number of destination VMs on NUMA machine. For each client VM, we choose 3Kpps and 6Kpps TCP STREAMs for packet generation rate of medium and heavy traffic, respectively. We report the packet receive rate improvements over the baseline NUMA node-aware policy, as shown in Figure 4-14.

We can observe that vFlowComb achieves an average of 20% more packet receive rate than the NUMA node-aware scheduling policy. The high-speed NIC can clearly reveal the bottlenecks in the NFV data plane. Under these circumstances, vFlowComb can intelligently place threads in the flow data path that minimizes the end-to-end performance slowdown. Interestingly, in the scenario with heavy traffic and small packet size (6Kpps, 256B), the performance improvement of vFlowComb drops when increasing the number of VMs. This is because this traffic poses a significant challenge to the I/O subsystem, creating a CPU time slice discontinuity.

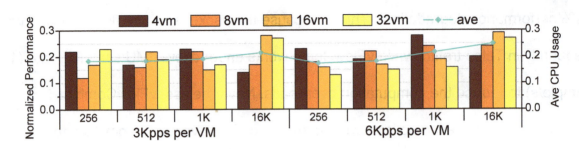

Figure 4-14.   Performance improvements over NUMA aware policy under extremely high throughput traffics.

We explore the thread mapping decision distributions under varying system traffic loads and co-located contentions to further demonstrate the correlation between thread mapping decisions and system traffic/contention status. We collect the scheduling decisions statistics for each mapping pattern listed in Figure 4-4. As shown in Figure 4-15A, we notice that the distribution of mapping E is mainly adopted in the medium traffic scenarios where ksoftirq is placed on a NIC node. The mappings F and G are adopted when the traffic load increases. In these situations, vFlowComb frequently schedules ksoftirq and vhost-net to destination VM nodes to avoid the expensive inter-socket communication at ksoftirq-vhost and vhost-VM stages.

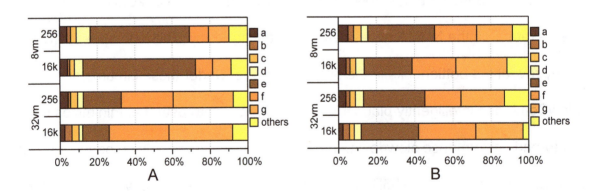

Figure 4-15.   Thread mapping decision distribution under different traffic loads, A) without contention, B) with contention.

We then introduce co-located contention delve deeper into the thread scheduling trends of vFlowComb. We deploy 4 single-node GraphAnalytic VMs on the NUMA machine to stress the memory subsystem. To create an irregular memory access pattern, we do not pin vCPUs to specific pCPU cores. As shown in Figure 4-15B, the mapping decisions are mainly balanced among configuration E, F, and G, since contention occurs irregularly on different NUMA sockets.

4.5.2 Overhead Analysis

We evaluate the overheads of DPBM based CTS mechanism. We first evaluate the computation overhead of our DPBM algorithm with various core and NIC hardware queue numbers. In this case, we assume that the ksoftirq core pool and vhost core pool are identical in size. We explore the performance of DPBM using TCP STREAM (3Kpps) and reg-dereg (250 call/s) respectively.

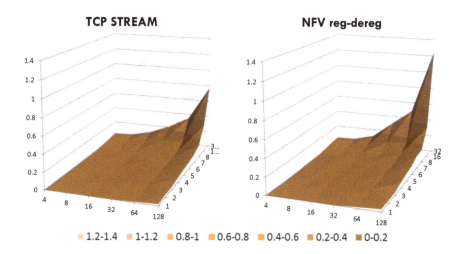

Figure 4-16.   Computational overheads of our DPBM with various NFV.

As shown in Figure 4-16, we can observe that the DPBM-based CTS can achieve optimal thread mappings within 0.77s (TCP STREAM) and 1.22s (NFV workloads) in a standard SHVS configuration (128 cores, 32 NIC queues).

4.6 Key Learning of vFlowComb

NFV plays an important role in current Telco and cloud data centers. It relies heavily on the performance of commodity standard high volume servers. We observe the

93

processing style of these workloads manifests as a heterogeneous software pipeline, in which the traffic flows are sequentially processed by heterogeneous software components. We conduct intensive and extensive characterizations of NFV deployment on current NUMA-based SHVS using real world Telco workloads. Our experimental results indicate that HSP introduces heterogeneous performance slowdown at different stages (intra-stage performance slowdown). The intra-stage performance slowdown is jointly determined by inter-socket communication overheads and co-located contention. We build a performance slowdown estimation model that accurately evaluates the intra-stage and end-to-end performance slowdowns. We then design a collaborative thread scheduling mechanism that is tailored to thread mapping in HSP. It exploits a dynamic programming-based end-to-end performance slowdown estimation method that accurately maps threads in the NFV data plane to improve traffic throughput (on average 23%) and increase the CPU utilization (7%) with negligible overhead (decision making time less than 1s).

CHAPTER 5
TOWARDS FULL CONTAINERIZATION IN CONTAINERIZED NETWORK FUNCTION VIRTUALIZATION

With exploding traffic is stuffing existing network infrastructure, today's telecommunication and cloud service providers resort to Network Function Virtualization (NFV) for greater agility and economics. Pioneer service provider such as AT&T proposes to adopt container in NFV to achieve shorter Virtualized Network Function (VNF) provisioning time and better runtime performance. However, we characterize typical NFV workloads on the containers and find that the performance is unsatisfactory. We observe that the shared host OS network stack is the main bottleneck, where the traffic flow processing involves a large amount of intermediate memory buffers and results in significant last level cache pollution. Existing OS memory allocation policies fail to exploit the locality and data sharing information among buffers.

In this chapter, we propose NetContainer, a software framework that achieves fine-grained hardware resource management for containerized NFV platform. NetContainer employs a cache access overheads guided page coloring scheme to coordinately address the inter-flow cache access overheads and intra-flow cache access overheads. It maps the memory buffer pages that manifest low cache access overheads (across a flow or among the flows) to the same last level cache partition. NetContainer exploits a footprint theory based method to estimate the cache access overheads and a Min-Cost Max-Flow model to guide the memory buffer mappings. We implement the NetContainer in Linux kernel and extensively evaluate it with real NFV workloads. Experimental results show that NetContainer outperforms conventional page coloring-based memory allocator by 48% in terms of successful call rate.

5.1 Containerized NFV

Pioneer service providers such as AT&T, Deutsche Telekom [78], and British Telecommunication [79] are turning to lightweight virtualization technology, such as Linux Container to resort to swift service provisioning for their NFV adoption. Doing so, Telco service provider can establish micro-services architecture that connects across multiple containers to implement the on-demand resource accesses on a more real-time basis than virtual machine based technology. The telecom service scalability could be greatly enhanced by container-based technology since it is possible to scale up a service by distributing thousands of containers in a short time.

Nevertheless, the container based NFV is not a free lunch. To retain the backward compatibility, current container based VNFs have to rely on kernel's networking functions such as Firewall/ Netfilter, IPsec NAT, and the most important, cgroups/ sendfile/splice mechanism which is the fundamental technique for Linux containers. Though recent efforts [80] attempted to avoid data copy by implementing a custom-built user-level TCP stack, and achieved the improved performance, they do not fully support all kernel functionalities.

We conduct intensive characterization by consolidating containerized NFV workloads on modern COTS servers, and our experimental results paint a frustrating picture—the network throughput/latency of containerized NFV is inferior to the performance of state-of-the-art virtualization based NFV setup with DPDK acceleration. In our experiment, we use Clearwater [67], a typical Telco NFV workload of growing importance in AT&T and Verizon data centers. The Telco NFV workloads have more strict Quality-of-Service (QoS) requirements than traditional web serving workloads [81] and transaction processing. The successful call rate (i.e. a metric that indicates the QoS of the calling system) of the containerized platform is lower than virtualized platform by 27%. To understand the root causes of the performance overheads in the kernel-sharing containerized NFV, we study the flow connection locality, memory/cache allocation, and Linux control group management of the container-based packet processing on a COTS server. Our characterization experiences reveal that current containerized environment lacks the support for fine-grained hardware resource isolation for NFV workloads. The memory buffer allocation is arbitrary, and cache mapping is decoupled with memory buffer allocation.

Modern NFV traffic is bursty. Considering the NFV packet processing involves a large amount of intermediate memory buffer, the packet processing of concurrent flows can evict the data to-be-used by other flows in the cache and pollute the cache with their own data, while this data may get evicted by other flows very soon. The cache thrashing caused by evicting and reloading data and data structures among multiple flows can significantly degrade the throughput and incur tail latency for certain flows. The random page allocation policy of the network memory buffers is the root cause of last level cache pollution. In current policy, the newly allocated memory pages are randomly mapped to un-selected cache regions. This approach fails to exploit any locality and data sharing information among specific intermediate buffers, and restricts the opportunity to establish a fine-grained hardware resource management in modern containerized NFV platform.

In this chapter, we propose NetContainer, a software framework that achieves a fine-grained hardware resource management for containerized NFV platform. We design a cache access overheads guided page coloring scheme, in which the inter-flow cache access overheads and intra-flow cache access overheads are coordinately addressed.

NetContainer sorts the memory buffer pages in groups where each group manifests near-optimized cache access overheads (across a flow or among the flows). NetContainer then maps these groups to the separate last level cache partitions using page coloring technique. By doing so, the cache pollution is mitigated since data with low locality is avoided to share the same cache region. In the meantime, the system throughput is guaranteed since the cache contention within the same color is minimized by selecting the buffer pages with high data locality. To achieve this goal, NetContainer employs two novel techniques.

First, NetContainer exploits the footprint theory and Miss Ratio Curve (MRC) [82-85] to model the cache access overheads of each intermediate memory buffer in the system. The cache access overhead will be quantified by this model and used as the guidance for the cache mapping algorithm. Second, NetContainer innovatively models the cache mapping problem into a classical Minimum Cost/Maximum Flow (MCMF) problem. The memory buffers and different cache colors are mapped as vertices in a bipartite graph. The edges between memory buffer vertices and cache set vertices are weighted by the cache access overheads, which are also the costs between vertices. So our problem is to find the solution with minimum cost (least cache access overheads) and maximum flow (highest throughput as possible). We also design related schemes to handle the various flow priorities and cache color budget tuning.

We implement the NetContainer based on Linux kernel 4.1. Evaluation results show that NetContainer improves the successful call rates by 34% on average and up to 48% when running typical NFV workloads. This suggests that the concurrency is improved significantly.

5.2 Backgrounds and Motivation

5.2.1 Virtualization of Telco Workloads

The telecommunication services are conventionally deployed on application-specific hardware. Since the carrier-grade systems running in Telco data center should provide high availability and fast resilience, the telecom service infrastructures are commonly over-provisioned to handle the service peak and high availability requirements. The network function virtualization is to run telecom services on virtual machines or containers so as to provide the elastic and scalable service deployment.

A typical Telco service is IP Multimedia Subsystem (IMS). IMS provides session control for IP-based voice, video, and messaging services based on Session Initiation Protocol (SIP). A typical IMS service includes functionality for End User authentication and authorization, call control and charging for multimedia sessions, as well as QoS decision and notifications at data path level through the integration with core network platforms.

SIP is an Internet standard protocol for establishing and managing multimedia sessions. It is a protocol of growing importance with uses in Voice over Internet Protocol (VoIP), instant messaging, IP television, and voice and video conferencing. It is also the basis for the IMS standard for the Third Generation Partnership Project. The voice over Internet protocol (VoIP) access and SIP services in the North American market grew 23.7%, 25.2% in terms of installed users and revenue, respectively. SIP is designed to handle control messages (e.g., session creation or termination) and is referred to as a control-plane protocol. The transfer of the actual session data relies on a separate data-plane protocol such as TCP and UDP. Compared to TCP or UDP, SIP has stronger quality-of-service (QoS) requirements that complicate its performance characteristics

than other protocols. A typical TCP-based SIP processing flow with essential

intermediate buffers is shown in Figure 5-1.

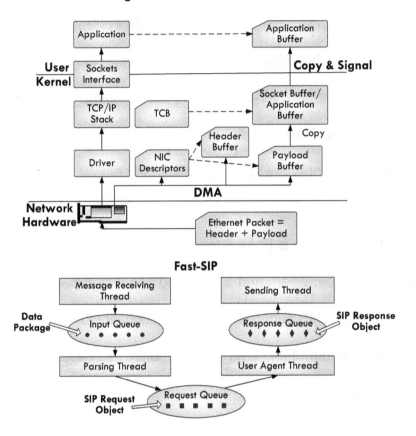

Figure 5-1.   TCP based SIP processing flow.

5.2.2 Network Function Virtualization using Containers

Operating system level virtualization virtualizes the operating system kernel in a

way such that applications running on shared kernel are unaware of other competitors.

On Linux such kind of virtualization is called Linux Container. Containers use Linux

control groups (cgroups) to limit the resources of user-land processes. Linux network

namespaces provides the network isolation by associating a private network stack for

each container and enabling it a limited view of the networking, file system and process

trees. As shown in Figure 5-2. Packets traverse the namespace boundary by means of

100

veth pairs, which are a pair of interfaces connected through a pipe: packets inserted in one end are received on the other end. By probing the two ends of the veth pipe in different namespaces, packets can be moved from one network namespace to another. In addition, a vSwitch connects all the veth interfaces in the host namespace among each other and with the physical network.

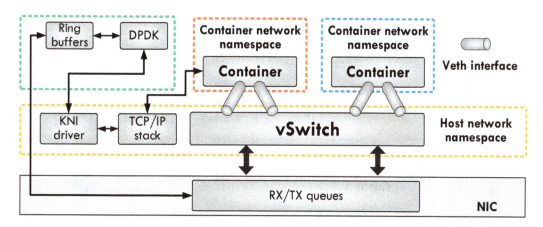

Figure 5-2.   DPDK enabled container networking.

The Intel DPDK platform is designed to allow user space applications to directly poll the NIC for data. It uses huge pages to pre-allocate memory pool (mempool), and then DMA incoming packets directly into these pages. In particular, the DPDK kernel NIC Interface (KNI) allows userspace applications access to the Linux kernel network stack. We show a typical flow of KNI access in Figure 5-2. For the incoming packets that need to access the kernel network stack, the packets should be copied from userspace buffer m_buf to kernel space buffer sk_buff during this process.

5.2.3 Page Coloring

The page coloring technique is used in modern operating system to control the mappings of physical memory pages to specific cache sets. Memory pages that are mapped to the same cache regions are painted the same color. Modern shared Last Level Cache (LLC) is physically indexed and set associative. OS uses the most

101

significant bits of a physical address as the physical page number. When the address is used in a cache lookup operation, it is divided into a Tag, a Cache Index and a Cache offset as shown in Figure 5-3. The page offset usually overlaps with the least-significant cache index bits, leaving several common bits between the cache set index and the physical page number. These bits are referred to as cache color. Cache sets with the same color value in their cache set indexes form a cache region.

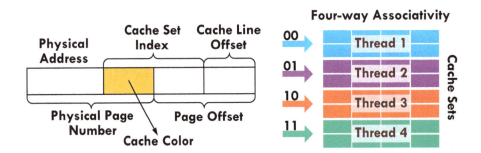

Figure 5-3.   Page coloring technique.

5.3 Characterizing Containerized NFV

We characterize the memory and cache access pattern of NFV workloads in container based platform. We first describe our experimental setup. We then present the architectural overheads analysis for NFV workloads to identify the main bottlenecks. After that, we continue to explore the impacts of different memory page/cache mappings to the performance of NFV system. Finally, we detailed investigate the locality and data sharing characteristics of the critical intermediate buffers across the NFV data processing flow.

5.3.1 Experimental Setup

Hardware Platform Our physical platform configuration is shown in Table 5-1. The system uses four Intel X520 SPF+ 10 Gigabit Ethernet NICs divided into two groups and are associated with two NUMA nodes respectively. To eliminate the NUMA effects, the core affinity and cache coloring are all considered within single socket.

Table 5-1.   Platform configurations

Item	Value
COTS system	SuperMicro 8048B, 4-socket NUMA
Processor	Intel Xeon E7-4809 v2, 1.9GHz (IvyBridge) 6 physical cores (12 Threads)/socket 12MB L3 cache for each socket, fully associative 64KB L1 cache and 256KB L2 cache for each core
Memory	64GB, DDR3 for each socket, 256GB in total
Interconnection	Intel QuickPath Interconnect, 6.4GT/s
NIC	Intel X540 10GBase-T, Mellanox 40GB SFP+ Associate with socket 0 and 4

Software Platform and Workloads We use Docker [86] as our container management and orchestration platform. Our test platform runs Ubuntu 14.04. In this paper, we use network intensive micro-benchmark Netperf [71] to generate TCP STREAM as stable and controllable traffic loads. We also use carrier-grade SIP-based IMS services Clearwater [67] as NFV service cluster. Clearwater serves as a system that registers the locations of virtual user clients at proxy-registrar server and lets them make phone calls to another user. Clearwater consists of a series of typical function components with various resource utilization patterns in a Telco data center, and could be easily deployed as VNFs in NFV environment.

Bono is a scalable edge proxy in the NFV environment. It serves as a gateway and provides connections to the Clearwater system for clients. Sprout processes the incoming requests from Bono, acting as a registrar and authoritative routing proxy. The Sprout cluster includes a Memcached cluster to store client registration data. Homestead provides web services interface to Sprout for retrieving authentication credentials and user profile information; providing a subscriber server and employs Cassandra as the backing store for its managed data. We deploy each service (Bono, Sprout, Homestead) as a container. In Clearwater, the Bono, Sprout and Homestead components constitute a basic service function chain. We can increase the number of instances for different components for scaling out.

Clients traffic generation We use the SIPp [68] to generate real world Telco NFV traffic. It is a performance-testing tool for Telco infrastructure and can establish and release multiple calls to an IMS NFV cluster. We choose user registration and deregistration (reg-dereg) calls for the traffic flow in this paper. A reg-dereg call consists of three requests: one for registration, one for authentication, and one for deregistration. SIPp initiates each call with an initiated call rate. If a response to a request times out (10s), the call will be tagged as failed. SIPp initiates call with an initiated call rate. Each trial of experiment runs for 300s. We run 5 trials and take the average results. We use the Successful Call Rate (SCR), which is used as an indicator of the service quality of the NFV system.

5.3.2 Processing Overheads Analysis

We instrument the processing time of primary functional elements in containerized TCP-based SIP workloads using Oprofile [87]. We group all functions along a typical processing flow into functional elements as follows: driver, buffer conversion, KNI copy, TCP protocol, system call, SIP queue conversion, and others. We present the per-packet processing time breakdown by varying the VNF number of a service chain in Figure 5-4. We vary the number of instances and consolidate different component configurations on 1 server. Each instance is assigned with 1 physical core (2 threads). The configurations are as follow: 1 Bono; 1 Bono-1 Sprout; 1 Bono-1 Sprout-1

104

Homestead; 1 Bono-2 Sprout-1 Homestead; 1 Bono-2 Sprout-2 Homestead. In this experiment, the I/Os larger than MTU are segmented into several Ethernet packets.

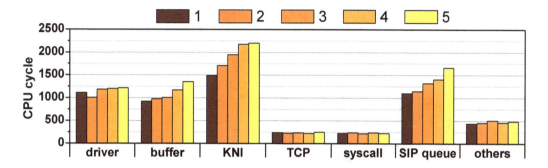

Figure 5-4.   Processing time breakdown for SIP workloads.

The increasing VNF number leads to higher processing time due to resource contention. For each service chain, doubling the instances of Sprout and Homestead can improve the call capacity (at 90% successful call rate) by less than 30%. This is because of the overheads of synchronization and load balance between instances.

We observe that the buffer conversion/release, KNI data copy, and SIP queue conversion consume a large amount of processing time. Worse, these memory-related overheads increase as the VNF number grows. The overheads breakdown reveals that the NFV is memory intensive. It is worth to characterize NFV memory access feature and further explore the performance bottlenecks.

We further examine the impacts of last level cache (LLC) pollution on the multicore COTS server. We present an experiment to demonstrate the cache pollution problem caused by various memory buffer accesses in the NFV deployment. In the experiment, we deploy three Clearwater components (Bono, Sprout, Homestead) in separate containers to build a service chain and test them with SIP workloads. Each container is pinned to exclusive CPU core. We vary the input call number (100 call/s~700 call/s) to intensify the memory buffer allocations and cache accesses. We report the NFV performance using the successful call rate, and the last level cache misses per kilo-instruction, as shown in Figure 5-5.

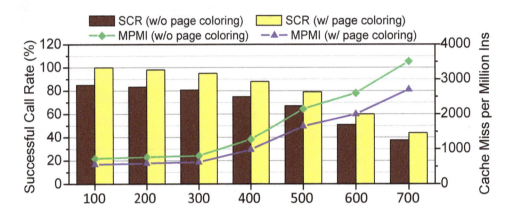

Figure 5-5.   SCR and cache miss w/ and w/o page coloring.

We can observe that with the increase of input call rate, the MPMI increases accordingly since the increasing call rates bring intensive network memory buffer allocations (KNI packet header copy, global TCB lookup, memory allocation in SIP stacks, etc.). Since the memory buffer accesses of different connections have weak data locality, the data cached for one connection is frequently evicted by other connections. The cache misses per million instructions increase by 2700 when input call rate reaches 700 call/s, while the successful call rate decreases to 44%.

Prior studies explore to reduce performance degradation using page coloring [88]. We make an initial attempt to increase the NFV system performance using page coloring as well. In our experiment, we map all the buffer pages belong to the same flow to the same cache color so as to isolate the cache pollution among different flows. We can observe that the improvement of SCR after applying page coloring.

Finding: Buffer conversion and release contribute to the most of the LLC miss. Isolating the buffer conversion from other operations in the LLC improves the system performance.

106

5.3.3 A Glimpse of Buffer Mapping Policies

We continue to explore if there exist other buffer/cache mapping policies can benefit performance under various flow patterns. We compare two representative buffer/cache mapping policies and examine their impacts to the system throughput and latency under different workloads setups. Our goals are twofold. First, to identify the overheads exist in conventional mapping policies. Second, to explore how to map memory buffer data-flow graph to different cache colors so as to maximize the performance, and explore the opportunity that can combine the benefits in both policies. We examine two general mapping policies, as shown in Figure 5-6.

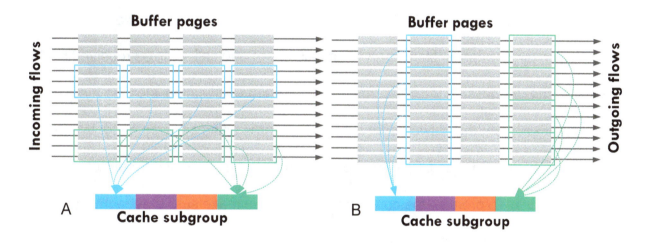

Figure 5-6.   Intermediate buffer clustering policies, A) Flow-based clustering. B) Element-based clustering.

Element-based clustering: In this setup, the memory buffers belong to the same stage of data-flow graph will be mapped to the same cache region. (i.e. the partitioned data-flow graph are mapped to different cache regions.) With the increase of flow number, the overflow memory buffers can be mapped to other cache colors.

Flow-based clustering: In this setup, the memory buffers belong to the same flow will be mapped to the same cache color. In essence, all the flows will be split into different flow groups and be mapped to different cache regions. The grouping policy could be various.

The element-based clustering takes advantage of inter-flow data locality, which indicates that the neighbour flows with high data locality will be grouped together. The flow-based clustering takes advantage of intra-flow data locality, which indicates that all required data will be grouped together.

We test these two mapping patterns using reg-dereg under two different SIP session locality configurations. In telecommunication, the SIP session locality is defined as most calls of a called user are initiated by a group of users. This is fairly common in telecommunication scenarios. In the high session locality configuration, we set 50 calls are received by one callee. Hence, an input call rate of 500 call/s will be received by 10 callees. In the low session locality configuration, we set each callee is called by one caller. We implement these two buffer mapping patterns using page coloring. We modify the Linux slab allocator and DPDK mempool allocator to implement different page coloring policies. To promise the connection locality, we make sure that each flow will be processed by the same core throughout its lifetime.

Figure 5-7 reports the successful call rates of two mapping patterns under different session locality configurations. Figure 5-7B shows that the element-based clustering benefits from high session locality more than flow-based clustering does (element-based has higher SCR than flow-based does), while the Figure 5-7A showing that it performs worse than flow-based clustering in a scenario with low session locality.

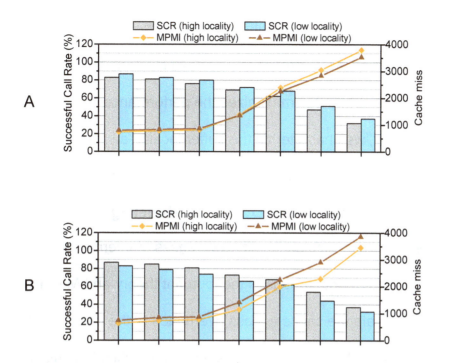

Figure 5-7.   Successful call rates of two mapping patterns under different session locality configurations, A) Flow-based clustering (high locality: 50 callers to 1 callee; low locality: 1 caller to 1 callee) B) Element-based clustering.

We discuss two simple yet representative cases. Extending these two scenarios to a more complex traffic pattern that includes multiple buffer elements will lead to a larger design space for the buffer mapping policies. These could be element-based, flow-based, or hybrid (e.g. where some portions of the buffers in a flow are clustered with buffers of other flows, while these buffers do not belong to the same stage).

These findings motivate us to design a decision process that takes account of: (1) a last level cache profile; (2) an intermediate buffer profile; (3) a profile of data locality among these intermediate buffers. The decision process outputs which buffer(s) should be allocated to each colored cache set. Specifically, the last level cache profile should specify the set of available resources (e.g., number of available colors, number of cores, cache sizes, etc.). The intermediate buffer profile should specify the data-flow graph of current buffer distribution, and the locality-awareness of each element buffer in the

109

data-flow graph. The decision process should compare all the possible buffer/cache mapping patterns (element-based clustering, flow-based clustering, or any combination of the two) and choose the option that maximizes the performance of NFV system.

To achieve this goal, we characterize the buffer locality-awareness and then propose a performance model to estimate the overheads of different mapping patterns.

5.4 Cache Access Overheads Modeling

We first characterize the session locality-awareness of intermediate buffers. We then propose a performance model that uses the footprint theory and Miss Ratio Curve (MRC) [82-84, 89] to estimate the cache access overheads of the intermediate memory buffers in the system. The cache access overhead will be quantified by this model and used as the guidance for the cache mapping decision-making process.

5.4.1 Locality Analysis of Memory Buffers

We characterize the session locality awareness of critical intermediate buffers across the flow processing path.

TCP/IP Header Buffer After the SKB conversion being initiated by KNI, the packet header data is copied into the header buffer. A typical TCP/IP header is around 40 Bytes to 128 Bytes [90], and the accesses to the header may result in one or more cache misses. Once the packet headers get processed, the cache will evict them and make room for new incoming headers. We can observe the packet header buffer has weak temporal locality. In the transmission-side processing, the situation is similar. The protocol stack creates header fields for the packet, and the packet is copied to user-space memory pool through KNI.

Payload Buffer Payload represents the meaningful application data in a TCP/IP packet. For a regular Ethernet frame size of 1514 bytes, the size of the payload is 1460

110

bytes. KNI module in the kernel copies the Payload data into a network stack memory buffer. The stack needs to copy this data into either a userland VNF buffer. Since the source buffer for the copy operation is in memory and the destination buffer may or may not be in the cache, several memory accesses are needed to complete the copy operation. Hence, the payload shows weak temporal locality.

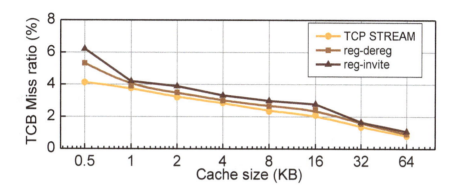

Figure 5-8.   TCB miss ratio v.s. various cache sizes.

TCP/IP Control Block Buffer TCB is a per-session data structure. TCP/IP stores its TCP session states in TCB and accesses it on the TCP critical path. Since the TCB is based on session instead of packet, we can expect a friendly cache locality as the packets from the same session access the same TCB. To understand the cache locality of TCB buffer, we simulate the TCB miss rates under various cache sizes. We exclude other pages from certain cache colors, and only map TCB pages to certain colors. We increase the cache size and report the TCB miss ratios in Figure 5-8. We observe that the reduction of miss ratio slows down twice beyond 1KB and 32KB, respectively. This indicates that TCBs exhibit cache locality across multiple packets, and the locality is quite dependent on the number of back-to-back packets processed for a connection.

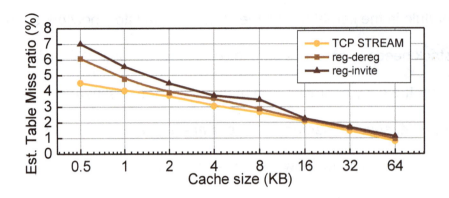

Figure 5-9.   Global listen/establish table miss ratio v.s. various cache sizes.

Global TCB Hash Table In current Linux kernel, the TCP connection

establishment and termination operations are managed in two global TCB hash tables,

namely the listen table and the established table. Each application process has its own

listen socket, and all the listen sockets are linked to a global bucket list in the listen table.

When there is an incoming TCP connection, the kernel has to traverse the bucket list to

choose a listen socket for this connection. We also characterize the hash node miss ratio

under different cache sizes and report the results in Figure 5-9. We can observe a cache

locality in global TCB Hash Table.

5.4.2 Cache Access Overheads Estimation Model

We build the performance model that estimates the cache sharing overheads of a

group of intermediate buffers based on footprint theory. The reuse distance analysis is

widely used in performance prediction and optimization of storage and CPU cache by

characterizing temporal locality of workloads. Given a reference trace of a program,

accurate miss ratio curves (MRCs) can be calculated by measuring reuse distance.

Using footprint theory, the cache sharing overhead by any group of intermediate buffers

is expected to be inferred from the footprint of each buffer. The cache access overheads estimation model can therefore generate the best buffer grouping that manifests the minimum cache sharing overheads without exhaustive trial-and-error tests.

Xiang et al. propose footprint theory [82, 83] to use reuse time instead of reuse distance to model the workloads and reduce the run-time overhead of MRC measurement to $O(N)$. Our model is derived from this model. It first measures the footprint fp of a program (i.e. flow processing operation at certain NFV stage in our case). It then uses the footprint to derive the lifetime lf, miss ratio mr, and reuse distance rd. Finally the cache sharing overhead could be predicted by combining fp and rd.

Calculating the Footprint A footprint measures the amount of data accessed within a time window, which is the time range in the memory trace. Let W be the set of $\binom{n}{2}$ windows of a length-n memory trace. A window $w = <l, s>$ has a window length l presents its footprint as s. Let $I(p)$ be a boolean function returning 1 when a predicate p is true and 0 otherwise. The footprint function $fp(l)$ averages over all windows of the same length l. There are $n - l + 1$ footprint windows of length l. We have the footprint function as:

$$fp(l) = \frac{\sum_{w_i \in W} s_i I(l_i = l)}{n - l + 1} \tag{5-1}$$

Converting Footprint to Miss Ratio Our ultimate goal is to predict the miss ratio and guide the buffer re-grouping algorithm. Based on the higher-order theory of locality (HOTL) [83], the footprint could be converted to miss ratio $mr(c)$. We first get the lifetime of a program, which is the average time that the program takes to access the cache with a size of c. The lifetime function is defined as the inverse of the footprint function:

$$lf(c) = fp^{-1}(c) \qquad\qquad (5\text{-}2)$$

Then the miss ratio can be derived from lifetime function. The average time between two consecutive misses can be calculated by taking the difference between the lifetime of $c+1$ and c. Formally, let $mr(c)$ be the capacity miss ratio, $lf(c)$ be the lifetime, and $im(c)$ be the inter-miss time. The miss ratio can be calculated as:

$$mr(c) = \frac{1}{im(c)} = \frac{1}{lf(c+1) - lf(c)} \qquad\qquad (5\text{-}3)$$

The reuse distance is the number of distinct data elements accessed between this and the previous access to the same datum. The distribution of all reuse distances gives the capacity miss ratio of the program in caches of all sizes and can accurately estimate the effect of conflict misses in direct map and set-associative cache. The reuse distance can be calculated as:

$$rd(c) = mr(c + 1) - mr(c) \qquad\qquad (5\text{-}4)$$

Finally we can use the reuse distance and footprint to cooperatively estimate the cache sharing overheads [91, 92]. Let A,B be two memory buffers share the same cache region, the effect of B on the locality of A is: P(capacity miss by A when co-running with B) = P((A's reuse distance + B's footprint) > cache size). The reuse of datum a in memory buffer A changes from a cache hit to a cache miss when A runs alone changes to A,B run together. The model can predict this miss. It takes the reuse distance of a in A and adds the footprint of B to obtain the shared-cache reuse distance. The effect of cache interference, i.e. the additional misses due to sharing, can be computed from single-program statistics. This is known as the composable model because it uses a linear number of sequential tests to predict the performance of an exponential number of parallel co-runs [93].

We adopt hardware time-stamp counters to sample the footprints of each flow processing program that belongs to different intermediate buffers. To considerably reduce the memory trace collection overheads, we adopt a spatially-hashed sampling method [85]. For given memory buffer, we can use the method above to estimate its cache access overhead to any color region in LLC since the system has the global buffer mapping information.

5.5 NetContainer

We propose NetContainer, a page coloring-based network buffer clustering scheme that simultaneously takes account of the cache pollution and intra-color cache contention. The goal of NetContainer is to optimize the buffer allocation of packet-processing flows of NFV applications and achieve the maximum throughput and low latency.

The core idea of NetContainer is to establish a page coloring based network buffer/LLC mapping scheme. The network buffers (may belong to any stage of the flow or any flow) exhibit the lowest cache access overheads will be mapped to the cache sets with the same color to reduce the eviction of to-be-reused data. In the meantime, the network buffers exhibit the highest cache access overheads will be partitioned to different cache colors to reduce the cache pollution and tail latency effect. To achieve this goal, NetContainer innovatively transforms the buffer/cache allocation problem into a classical Minimum-Cost Maximum Flow (MCMF) problem.

NetContainer works in four phases. First, it uses an on-line trace sampling to calculate footprints and reuse distance of current flow processing programs and their associated buffer information. Second, it adopts footprint theory to predict the cache access overheads for each flow processing program. Third, it exploits the MCMF model to solve the best buffer mapping patterns. Fourth, it uses page coloring to apply the buffer mapping decisions. A workflow of NetContainer is shown in Figure 5-10.

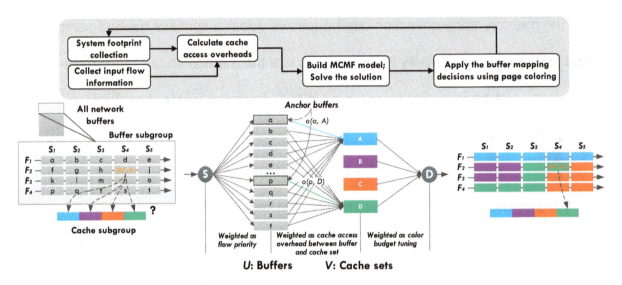

Figure 5-10.   An overview of NetContainer workflow.

5.5.1 Problem Formulation

Now we would like to answer the question that we have raised in 5.3: how should we cluster the right network buffers and map them into the right cache sets? We begin by introducing the system models. Consider m concurrent network data flows $F = \{F_1, F_2, ..., F_k, ..., F_m\}$. Each of the data flows, F_k, consists of n processing stages $S = \{S_1, S_2, ..., S_j, ..., S_n\}$. So we have $m \cdot n$ intermediate buffers $B = \{B_l (F_k, S_j) | F_k \in F, S_j \in S \}$ in the kernel network stack and VNF protocol stack. The last level cache supports c cache colors C_i. The cache access overhead from buffer B_l to cache C_i is $o(B_l (F_k, S_j), C_i)$.

The goal is to construct c network buffer groups, $FG = \{FG_1, FG_2, ..., FG_c\}$, and map each of them to a cache color C_i. Each buffer group FG_k consists of N_k network buffers, which could be chosen from any of the $B_l (F_k, S_j)$. Different buffer groups may

116

have different amounts of network buffers. In the meantime, the overall cache access overhead $o(FG_k, C_k)$ of each buffer group FG_k should be minimized.

We express the problem of optimally clustering network intermediate buffers as an instance of the classical min-cost maximum flow (MCMF) problem [47]. We also augment some necessary modification to enhance the scalability of MCMF problem. Figure 5-10 shows our modeling methodology. Since we assume we can quantify the cache access overhead for different buffer mappings (i.e. the cost of each edge in the MCMF problem), we can build a flow graph to solve the problem by finding the solution with lowest cost and the maximum flow throughput. As shown in Figure 5-10, the flow graph is designed as a bipartite graph $G= (U, V, E)$, where the left-hand set U denotes the set of all network memory buffers in an instantaneous snapshot of the system, and the right-hand set V denotes the set of all colors of the last level cache sets, with E denoting the possible mapping between buffer u and cache v. A flow that connects a unit in U and a unit in V could be treated as a scheduling decision for one network buffer. The weights of the edges between source node S and set U can be used to represent the priority of certain buffer groups. The weights of the edges between u and v denote the cache access overhead from buffer u to cache color v. The weights of the edges between V and sink node D can be reserved to tune the cache color budgets.

5.5.2 Solving the MCMF

Having obtained the basic MCMF flow graph, we need to find practical way to solve this problem since our application has high-performance demand. We find several challenges when MCMF is used in our problem space. First, the basic graph is a complete bipartite graph, which leads to a high degree for each vertex. Such a huge solution space is restrictive in a cache mapping application. Second, the overall cache

117

access overheads of a cluster may become hard to estimate since we use single cache access overhead to denote the weight of an edge. The correlation between different edges is non-trivial. An amendment must be added to estimate the overall cache access overhead of a buffer cluster. We represent the cost of the edge from u to v as a function.

To reduce the problem space and improve the efficiency, we split the input buffer area and candidate cache space into several subgroups and execute the MCMF optimization to each subgroup. As shown in Figure 5-10, the selected buffer subgroup consists of the buffers that are passed through by a portion of flows in an instantaneous snapshot. The destination cache sets are also the subgroup of available cache colors. Then the problem has been reduced from global optimization to a region-based optimization.

In the region-based optimization, we still have the same goal as in the global optimization. We first choose "anchor buffers" and directly map them to the candidate colors in the cache subgroup. The buffers with the least cache access overheads among each other will be chosen as anchor buffers. The rest of the buffers establish edges to all candidate cache colors, and the edges are weighted by corresponding cache access overhead. Using "anchor buffers" can increase the deterministic and further reduce the complexity of buffer clustering. Choosing the appropriate capacity of subgroup for buffers and caches has substantial impacts to the tradeoff between complexity and performance. A bigger subgroup may help to choose more accurate buffer cluster, while incurring longer decision time which may restrict its decision-making frequency.

The MCMF algorithm performs a search for the given flow graph, with respect to the cost assigned to each edge, subject to fairness constraints and maximum flow throughput. We choose the state-of-the-art solver [94] by Goldberg. The worst-case complexity bounds is $O(V \cdot E \cdot \log(V \cdot P) \log(V^2/E))$, where P is the largest absolute value of an edge cost. Under the circumstance that flows with different priorities, we can tune the cost on the edges from source node S to u to enable more conservative cache allocations for high priority-flows. For example, the total cost of high priority-flows could be weighted higher than low priority-flows, thus less high priority-flows shall share the same cache color.

5.6 Evaluation

We implement a prototype of NetContainer into Linux kernel 4.1. We evaluate NetContainer against various micro-benchmarks and real NFV workloads on modern COTS server. We vary the traffic loads intensities and session localities to validate the effectiveness. We then demonstrate the zoomed system analysis and discuss the design space in NetContainer.

5.6.1 Methodology

NFV environment The test scenarios are designed to mimic real service chains in NFV deployment, as shown in Figure 5-11. Each service chain consists of no more than 3 VNFs. All VNFs are deployed as Docker images on test COTS server. We set up 4 dedicated servers (2 clients and 2 receivers). Each server is connected to a 10GB NIC. We deploy 32 VMs on the clients and receivers as traffic generators and traffic sinks, respectively. They can generate a maximum of 32 SIPp call initiators, which can be processed by 8 service chains. The traffic flows are processed by containerized VNFs in the service chain in tandem through the virtual switches.

119

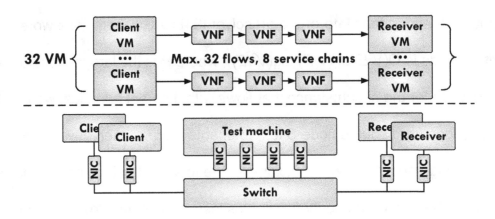

Figure 5-11.   NFV environment setup for evaluation.

NFV Workloads We evaluate NetContainer using TCP traffic and Telco NFV traffic. For TCP traffic, we set all VNFs as packet forwarding components. For real NFV traffic, the VNFs are deployed as Clearwater components, as described in 5.3. We generate heavy and medium traffics by tuning the packet generation rate (packet per second) at the SIPp call initiators. At each client VM, we use Netperf to generate 512B TCP_STREAM traffic at 24Kpps (medium) and 32Kpps (heavy). We use a small packet size to maximize the system stress. For the NFV workload reg-dereg, we set the input call rate of SIPp call initiator as 300 call/s (medium) and 500 call/s (heavy). For reg-invite, we set the input call rate of SIPp call initiator as 100 call/s (medium) and 150 calls/s (heavy). We also define the session locality for NFV workloads as high locality (50 callers to 1 callee) and low locality (1 caller to 1 callee). We list traffic configurations in Table 5-2.

Experimental Variables We test all three traffic loads (TCP STREAM, reg-dereg, and reg-invite) under various input traffic capacity, VNF number in the service chain, and session locality. We vary the input traffic capacity by changing the packet per second and concurrent input flow number. We vary the VNF numbers in a service chain in different ways. For TCP traffic, we change the length of the service chain by adding or

120

reducing the number of packet forwarding VNFs. For the Telco traffics, we change the

VNF number by consolidating more or less Clearwater function modules on the

remaining VNFs. The session locality can only be changed in NFV workloads. We can

control the network communication pattern (which clients to which servers) in the

Clearwater setup. We use 12 colors in this evaluation.

Table 5-2. Platform configurations

		TCP_STREAM	*reg-dereg*	*reg-invite*
Traffic	Medium	24K pps @ 512B	300 call/s	100 call/s
	Heavy	32K pps @ 512B	500 call/s	150 call/s
Locality	Low	1 client to 1 server	1 caller to 1 callee	
	High	4 clients to 1 server	50 callers to 1 callee	

Baseline scheduling policy We use 4 baseline memory allocators. A. The Linux

slab memory allocator; B. The utility-based partitioning [95]. C. The element-based

clustering method. D. The flow-based clustering method. The last two policies were

described in 5.3.

5.6.2 Overall Benefits

To show the effectiveness of NetContainer in reducing LLC pollution and handling

tail latency, we run NFV workloads (reg-dereg and reg-invite) under various VNF

numbers (from 1 to 3), various traffic intensities and various session localities (as shown

in Table 5-2). We report the Successful Call Rate (SCR) and LLC miss (MPKI) in Figure

5-12.

From Figure 5-12 we can draw several key insights that show the benefits of

NetContainer. In all scenarios, we observe that NetContainer outperforms other

baselines in terms of SCR and LLC miss rate. Though the LLC miss ratio are not

significantly improved in some scenarios, we can always expect at least 17% SCR improvement brought by NetContainer. Note that NetContainer considerably

outperforms peer memory allocators in high locality scenario.

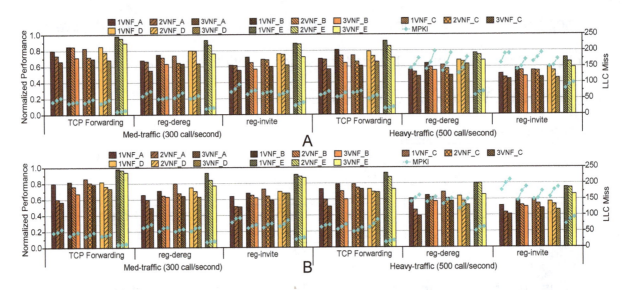

Figure 5-12.   Normalized performance, A) Low session locality. B) High session locality.

When there are 3 VNFs in the service chain, all four baselines suffer significant

performance degradations. Baseline B performs slightly better than other peers since

both Baseline C and D are not optimal under such long data-flow pipeline. Nevertheless,

NetContainer is still able to avoid performance degradation by finding the best memory

buffer mapping with the least cache pollution and contention.

The successful call rate is determined by the request response time. Both

reg-dereg and reg-invite are TCP traffics with mixed packet sizes. In medium traffic

scenarios, NetContainer demonstrates about 21% more successful call rate than other

baselines. When the input call rate is increased, NetContainer gains 34% on average

and up to 48% more successful calls than other baselines on average.

5.6.3 Benefits of Locality-aware Cache Partition

We continue to examine how tail latency workloads benefit from our session

locality-aware cache partition feature. In this test, we run reg-dereg and reg-invite with

NetContainer and other four baselines with medium and heavy input traffic. We set the VNF number as 1. We tune the session locality of input workloads and report the average and worst call waiting time in Figure 5-13. We can draw key insights as follows.

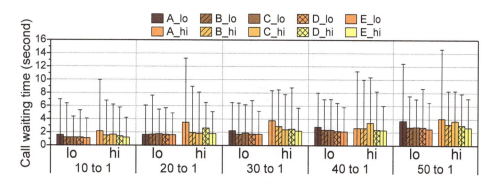

Figure 5-13.   Average call waiting time (bar, lower is better) and worst call waiting time (whisker).

When the session locality and input traffic are both relatively low, the average waiting time for baselines and NetContainer do not differ too much. NetContainer clearly has lower average waiting time and worst waiting time when the input traffic is heavy. With the increase of session locality, NetContainer keeps gaining low average and worst waiting time whenever the medium and heavy input traffic, while the baselines perform poor at heavy traffics since they cannot capture the accurate buffer locality information, therefore cannot map highly contentious memory pages to different cache regions.

5.6.4 Benefits of Locality-aware Buffer Clustering

We further explore how NFV workloads benefit from our 2-D buffer locality-aware clustering feature. In this test, we run reg-dereg and reg-invite with NetContainer and other four baselines under heavy input traffic. We set the VNF number as 2 and set the session locality of input workloads as 70 caller to 1 callee. We group all cache colors into five accumulative cache colors and report the normalized MPKI of each cumulative cache region in Figure 5-14. Since the MPKI of each baseline varies considerably, we

123

define a metric as normalized MPKI. For a given setup, the normalized MPKI equals to MPKI divided by average MPKI in this setup. Therefore a normalized MPKI can be used to measure the fluctuation of LLC miss distribution.

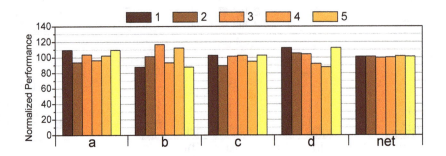

Figure 5-14.   Normalized MPKI of accumulative cache colors.

As shown in Figure 5-14, the cache miss rate of NetContainer is the least fluctuating comparing to other four baselines. This represents that the buffer pages are appropriately mapped to different cache regions, without incurring contention and under-utilization.

5.7 Key Learning of NetContainer

In this work, we characterize typical NFV workloads and software setup on containerized environment. Our characterization results show that current intermediate buffer pages mapping is not cache efficient in NFV service chain. Specifically, we observe that the NFV traffic flows manifest inter-flow and intra-flow data locality. Leveraging this multi-dimensional data locality, we observe an opportunity to group intermediate buffer pages to specific cache regions using page coloring technique to avoid cache pollution and reduce the cache contention in the same cache color. We propose NetContainer, a framework that achieves a fine-grained hardware resource management for containerized NFV platform. We design a cache access overheads guided page coloring scheme. It exploits the footprint theory to model the cache access overheads of each intermediate memory buffer in the system. It then models the cache

mapping problem into a classical minimum cost maximum flow (MCMF) problem. The

edges between memory buffer vertices and cache set vertices are weighted by the

cache access overheads, which are also the costs between vertices. Experimental

results show that NetContainer remarkably controls the cache pollution and cache

contention for latency-critical NFV workloads, and hence maintaining a stable

performance under various traffic intensities and session localities.

CHAPTER 6
CONCLUSIONS

This dissertation explores the opportunity and demonstrates the initial efforts on designing the comprehensive data center system for big data processing in IoT era. We point out two critical gaps at different layers that decouple the communication and computation functionalities in the IoT big data processing system. Facing with these challenges, we propose a cross-layer design that pins the intelligence to the communication path. As a two-dimensional solution, we first move the intelligence nearer to the data generation site to reduce the data transmission overheads and then pin the intelligence deeper into the network layer to make the communication path more intelligent. The proposed techniques enable the bright future for the IoT network system.

The future work will focus on designing the network system that is tailored to the edge/in-situ computing infrastructure. The design goals will meet the specific performance/power/latency requirements of edge computing. The delivered research will significantly improve the communication throughput and reduce the latency of future IoT in-situ data center.

LIST OF REFERENCES

[1] S. Lasluisa, F. Zhang, T. Jin, I. Rodero, H. Bui, and M. Parashar, "In-situ feature-based objects tracking for data-intensive scientific and enterprise analytics workflows," *Cluster Comput.*, pp. 29–40, 2015.

[2] W. Huang, M. Allen-Ware, J. B. Carter, E. Elnozahy, H. Hamann, T. Keller, C. Lefurgy, J. Li, K. Rajamani, and J. Rubio, "TAPO: Thermal-aware power optimization techniques for servers and data centers," in *Proc. International Green Computing Conference and Workshops*, 2011.

[3] D. Meisner and T. F. Wenisch, "DreamWeaver: Architectural support for deep sleep," in *Proc. Int. Conf. on Architectural Support for Programming Languages and Operating Systems*, 2012, pp. 313–324.

[4] V. Kontorinis, L. E. Zhang, B. Aksanli, J. Sampson, H. Homayoun, E. Pettis, D. M. Tullsen, and T. Simunic Rosing, "Managing distributed UPS energy for effective power capping in data centers," in *Proc. Int. Symp. Comput. Archit.*, 2012, pp. 488–499.

[5] M. Guevara, B. Lubin, and B. C. Lee, "Navigating heterogeneous processors with market mechanisms," in *Proc. IEEE 19th International Symposium on High-Performance Computer Architecture*, 2013, pp. 95–106.

[6] Y. Zhai, X. Zhang, S. Eranian, L. Tang, and J. Mars, "Happy: Hyperthread-aware power profiling dynamically," in *Proc. USENIX Annual Technical Conference*, 2014, pp. 211–217.

[7] D. Lo, L. Cheng, R. Govindaraju, L. A. Barroso, and C. Kozyrakis, "Towards energy proportionality for large-scale latency-critical workloads," in *Proc. International Symposium on Computer Architecture*, 2014, pp. 301–312.

[8] A. Putnam and Others, "A reconfigurable fabric for accelerating large-scale datacenter services," in *Proc. International Symposium on Computer Architecture*, 2014, pp. 13–24.

[9] M. Shah, P. Ranganathan, J. Chang, N. Tolia, D. Roberts, and T. Mudge, "Data dwarfs: Motivating a coverage set for future large data center workloads," in *Proc. Workshop Architectural Concerns in Large Datacenters*, 2010.

[10] D. Logothetis, C. Trezzo, K. C. Webb, and K. Yocum, "In-situ MapReduce for log processing," in *Proc. USENIX Annual Technical Conference*, 2011, pp. 115.

[11] L. Shi, W.-Z. Song, Y. Xie, Z. Peng, and J. Lees, "InsightTomo: In-Situ Seismic Tomographic Imaging System," in *Proc. The ACM Conference on Embedded Networked Sensor Systems*, 2014.

[12] H. Viswanathan, E. K. Lee, and D. Pompili, "Enabling real-time in-situ processing of ubiquitous mobile-application workflows," in *Proc. 2013 IEEE 10th International Conference on Mobile Ad-Hoc and Sensor Systems*, 2013, pp. 324–332.

[13] Í. Goiri, W. Katsak, K. Le, T. D. Nguyen, and R. Bianchini, "Parasol and GreenSwitch: Managing Datacenters Powered by Renewable Energy," in *Proc. of the Eighteenth International Conference on Architectural Support for Programming Languages and Operating Systems*, 2013, pp. 51–64.

[14] C. Li, R. Zhou, and T. Li, "Enabling distributed generation powered sustainable high-performance data center," in *Proc. International Symposium on High-Performance Computer Architecture*, 2013, pp. 35–46.

[15] C. Li, A. Qouneh, and T. Li, "iSwitch: Coordinating and optimizing renewable energy powered server clusters," in *Proc. International Symposium on Computer Architecture*, 2012, pp. 512–523.

[16] N. Sharma, S. Barker, D. Irwin, and P. Shenoy, "Blink: managing server clusters on intermittent power," *ACM SIGPLAN Notices*, vol. 46, no. 3, pp. 185–198, 2011.

[17] R. Singh, D. Irwin, P. Shenoy, and K. K. Ramakrishnan, "Yank: Enabling green data centers to pull the plug," in *Proc. 10th USENIX Symposium on Networked Systems Design and Implementation*, 2013, pp. 143–155.

[18] C. Li, Y. Hu, R. Zhou, M. Liu, L. Liu, J. Yuan, and T. Li, "Enabling datacenter servers to scale out economically and sustainably," in *Proc. 46th Annu. IEEE/ACM Int. Symp. Microarchitecture*, 2013, pp. 322–333.

[19] M. Arlitt, C. Bash, S. Blagodurov, Y. Chen, T. Christian, D. Gmach, C. Hyser, N. Kumari, Z. Liu, M. Marwah, and others, "Towards the design and operation of net-zero energy data centers," in *Proc. 13th IEEE Intersociety Conference on Thermal and Thermomechanical Phenomena in Electronic Systems,* 2012, pp. 552–561.

[20] I. Goiri, R. Beauchea, K. Le, T. D. Nguyen, M. E. Haque, J. Guitart, J. Torres, and R. Bianchini, "GreenSlot: Scheduling energy consumption in green datacenters," in *Proc. of 2011 International Conference for High Performance Computing, Networking, Storage and Analysis on - SC '11*, 2011, pp. 1–11.

[21] S. Govindan, A. Sivasubramaniam, and B. Urgaonkar, "Benefits and limitations of tapping into stored energy for datacenters," *ACM SIGARCH Comput. Archit. News*, vol. 39, no. 3, pp. 341-341-352–352, 2011.

[22] S. Govindan, D. Wang, A. Sivasubramaniam, and B. Urgaonkar, "Leveraging stored energy for handling power emergencies in aggressively provisioned datacenters," *ACM SIGPLAN Not.*, vol. 47, no. 4, pp. 75-75-75-86-86–86, 2012.

[23] L. Liu, C. Li, H. Sun, Y. Hu, J. Gu, T. Li, J. Xin, and N. Zheng, "HEB : Deploying and Managing Hybrid Energy Buffers for Improving Datacenter Efficiency and Economy," in *Proc. of the 42nd Annual International Symposium on Computer Architecture*, 2015, pp. 463–475.

[24] B. Aksanli, T. Rosing, and E. Pettis, "Distributed battery control for peak power shaving in datacenters," in *Proc. International Green Computing Conference*, 2013.

[25] L. Tang, J. Mars, N. Vachharajani, R. Hundt, and M. Lou Soffa, "The impact of memory subsystem resource sharing on datacenter applications," *ACM SIGARCH Computer Architecture News*, vol. 39, no. 3, p. 283, 2011.

[26] S. Blagodurov, S. Zhuravlev, A. Fedorova, and M. Dashti, "A Case for NUMA-aware Contention Management on Multicore Systems," in *Proc. 19th Int. Conf. Parallel Archit. Compil. Tech.*, 2010, pp. 557–558.

[27] M. Liu and T. Li, "Optimizing virtual machine consolidation performance on NUMA server architecture for cloud workloads," in *Proc. Int. Symp. Comput. Archit.*, 2014, pp. 325–336.

[28] A. Pesterev, J. Strauss, N. Zeldovich, and R. T. Morris, "Improving network connection locality on multicore systems," in *Proc. of the 7th ACM european conference on Computer Systems*, 2012, pp. 337-350.

[29] X. Lin and Y. Chen, "Scalable Kernel TCP Design and Implementation for Short-Lived Connections," in *Proc. Int. Conf. on Architectural Support for Programming Languages and Operating Systems*, 2016, pp. 339–352.

[30] K. K. Ram, A. L. Cox, M. Chadha, and S. Rixner, "Hyper-Switch: A Scalable Software Virtual Switching Architecture," in *Proc. USENIX Annu. Tech. Conf.*, 2013, pp. 13–24.

[31] J. Hwang, K. K. Ramakrishnan, and T. Wood, "NetVM: High Performance and Flexible Networking Using Virtualization on Commodity Platforms," in *Proc. 11th USENIX Symp. Networked Syst. Des. Implement.*, 2014, pp. 445–458.

[32] P. Ranganathan, S. Adve, and N. P. Jouppi, "Reconfigurable Caches and their Application to Media Processing," in *Proc. 27th Annu. Int. Symp. Comput. Archit.*, 2000, pp. 214–224.

[33] Y. Xie and G. H. Loh, "PIPP: promotion/insertion pseudo-partitioning of multi-core shared caches," in *Proc. of the 36th annual international symposium on Computer architecture*, 2009, vol. 37, no. 3, pp. 174–183.

[34] D. Sanchez and C. Kozyrakis, "Vantage: scalable and efficient fine-grain cache partitioning," in *Proc. 38th Annu. Int. Symp. Comput. Archit.*, 2011, pp. 57–68.

[35] R. Liu, K. Klues, S. Bird, S. Hofmeyr, K. Asanovi, and J. Kubiatowicz, "Tessellation: space-time partitioning in a manycore client OS," in *Proc. First USENIX Conf. Hot Top. parallelism*, 2009, pp. 10–10.

[36] D. Lo, L. Cheng, R. Govindaraju, P. Ranganathan, and C. Kozyrakis, "Heracles: Improving Resource Efficiency at Scale," in *Proc. of the 42nd Annual International Symposium on Computer Architecture*, 2015, pp. 450–462.

[37] R. Iyer, L. Zhao, F. Guo, R. Illikkal, S. Makineni, D. Newell, Y. Solihin, L. Hsu, and S. Reinhardt, "QoS policies and architecture for cache/memory in CMP platforms," *ACM SIGMETRICS Perform. Eval. Rev.*, vol. 35, no. 1, p. 25, 2007.

[38] H. Kasture and D. Sanchez, "Ubik: efficient cache sharing with strict qos for latency-critical workloads," in *Proc. Int. Conf. on Architectural Support for Programming Languages and Operating Systems*, 2014, pp. 729–742.

[39] B. Li, L. Zhao, R. Iyer, L. S. Peh, M. Leddige, M. Espig, S. E. Lee, and D. Newell, "CoQoS: Coordinating QoS-aware shared resources in NoC-based SoCs," *J. Parallel Distrib. Comput.*, vol. 71, no. 5, pp. 700–713, 2011.

[40] V. Seshadri, G. Pekhimenko, O. Ruwase, O. Mutlu, P. B. Gibbons, M. A. Kozuch, T. C. Mowry, and T. Chilimbi, "Page Overlays : An Enhanced Virtual Memory Framework to Enable Fine-grained Memory Management," in *Proc. 42nd Annu. Int. Symp. Comput. Archit.*, 2015, pp. 79–91.

[41] J. Mars, L. Tang, R. Hundt, K. Skadron, and M. Lou Soffa, "Bubble-Up: Increasing Utilization in Modern Warehouse Scale Computers via Sensible Co-locations," in *Proc. 44th Annu. IEEE/ACM Int. Symp. Microarchitecture*, 2011, p. 248.

[42] D. Novakovic, N. Vasic, and S. Novakovic, "Deepdive: Transparently identifying and managing performance interference in virtualized environments," in *Proc. USENIX Conf. Annu. Tech. Conf.*, 2013, pp. 219–230.

[43] N. Vasić, D. Novaković, S. Miučin, D. Kostić, and R. Bianchini, "DejaVu: accelerating resource allocation in virtualized environments," *ACM SIGARCH Comput. Archit. News*, vol. 40, no. 1, p. 423, 2012.

[44] C. Delimitrou and C. Kozyrakis, "Paragon: QoS-aware Scheduling for Heterogeneous Datacenters," in *Proc. of the 18th International Conference on Architectural Support for Programming Languages and Operating Systems*, 2013, pp. 77–88.

[45] C. Delimitrou and C. Kozyrakis, "Quasar: Resource-efficient and QoS-aware Cluster Management," in *Proc. of the 19th International Conference on Architectural Support for Programming Languages and Operating Systems*, 2014, pp. 127–144.

[46] Y. Hu, C. Li, L. Liu, and T. Li, "HOPE: Enabling Efficient Service Orchestration in Software-Defined Data Centers," in *Proc. of the 2016 International Conference on Supercomputing*, 2016, p. 10:1--10:12.

[47] M. Isard, V. Prabhakaran, J. Currey, U. Wieder, K. Talwar, and A. Goldberg, "Quincy : Fair Scheduling for Distributed Computing Clusters," *In Proc. of the ACM SIGOPS 22nd symposium on Operating systems principles*, 2009, pp. 261–276.

[48] J. Vlahos, "Surveillance Society: New High-Tech Cameras Are Watching You," *Popular Mechanics*, 2009.

[49] V. Kontorinis, L. E. Zhang, B. Aksanli, J. Sampson, H. Homayoun, E. Pettis, D. M. Tullsen, and T. Simunic Rosing, "Managing distributed UPS energy for effective power capping in data centers," in *Proc. International Symposium on Computer Architecture*, 2012, pp. 488–499.

[50] S. Fomel, P. Sava, I. Vlad, Y. Liu, and V. Bashkardin, "Madagascar: open-source software project for multidimensional data analysis and reproducible computational experiments," *J. Open Res. Softw.*, vol. 1, no. 1, p. e8, 2013.

[51] W. Burnett and S. Fomel, "Azimuthally anisotropic 3D velocity continuation," *Int. J. Geophys.*, vol. 2011, 2011.

[52] H. Kim and K. G. Shin, "Scheduling of battery charge, discharge, and rest," in *Proc. Real-Time Systems Symposium*, 2009, pp. 13–22.

[53] K. Yabuta, T. Matsushita, and T. Tsujikawa, "Examination of the cycle life of valve regulated lead acid batteries," in *Proc. International Telecommunications Energy Conference*, 2007, pp. 97–101.

[54] C. Bienia, S. Kumar, J. P. Singh, and K. Li, "The PARSEC benchmark suite: Characterization and architectural implications," in *Proc. of the International Conference on Parallel Architectures and Compilation Techniques*, 2008, pp. 72–81.

[55] S. Huang, J. Huang, J. Dai, T. Xie, and B. Huang, "The HiBench Benchmark Suite: Characterization of the MapReduce-Based Data Analysis," in *Proc. New Frontiers in Information and Software as Services: Service and Application Design Challenges in the Cloud*, 2011, pp. 209–228.

[56] M. Ferdman, A. Adileh, O. Kocberber, S. Volos, M. Alisafaee, D. Jevdjic, C. Kaynak, A. D. Popescu, A. Ailamaki, and B. Falsafi, "Clearing the clouds: a study of emerging scale-out workloads on modern hardware," in *Proc. of the seventeenth international conference on Architectural Support for Programming Languages and Operating Systems*, 2012, pp. 37–48.

[57] N. Femia, G. Petrone, G. Spagnuolo, and M. Vitelli, "Optimization of perturb and observe maximum power point tracking method," *IEEE Trans. Power Electron.*, vol. 20, no. 4, pp. 963–973, 2005.

[58] C. Cui, H. Deng, D. Telekom, U. Michel, and H. Damker, "Network functions virtualisation: An introduction, benefits, enablers, challenges and call for action," no. 1, pp. 1–16, 2012.

[59] ETSI ISG NFV. (2013). Network Functions Virtualisation (NFV): Architectural Framework.

[60] T. Koponen, K. Amidon, P. Balland, M. Casado, A. Chanda, B. Fulton, I. Ganichev, J. Gross, P. Ingram, E. Jackson, A. Lambeth, R. Lenglet, S.-H. Li, A. Padmanabhan, J. Pettit, B. Pfaff, R. Ramanathan, S. Shenker, A. Shieh, J. Stribling, P. Thakkar, D. Wendlandt, A. Yip, and R. Zhang, "Network Virtualization in Multi-tenant Datacenters," in *Proc. 11th USENIX Symp. Networked Syst. Des. Implement.*, 2014, pp. 203–216.

[61] (2016). Open Platform for NFV (OPNFV) [Online]. Available: https://www.opnfv.org/

[62] Intel. (2014). Intel® Open Network Platform Server Reference Architecture: SDN and NFV for Carrier-Grade Infrastructure and Cloud Data Centers.

[63] Y. Dong, X. Yang, X. Li, J. Li, K. Tian, and H. Guan, "High performance network virtualization with SR-IOV," in *Proc. IEEE 16th Int. Symp. High Perform. Comput. Archit., 2010*, pp. 1–10.

[64] Intel. Intel Data Direct I/O Technology (Intel DDIO): A Primer.

[65] W. Wang, J. W. Davidson, and M. Lou Soffa, "Predicting the Memory Bandwidth and Optimal Core Allocations for Multi-threaded Applications on Large-scale NUMA Machines," in *Proc. IEEE Int. Symp. High Perform. Comput. Archit.*, 2016, pp. 419–431.

[66] B. Pfaff, J. Pettit, T. Koponen, E. Jackson, A. Zhou, J. Rajahalme, J. Gross, A. Wang, J. Stringer, P. Shelar, K. Amidon, A. Networks, and M. Casado, "The Design and Implementation of Open vSwitch," in *Proc. 12th USENIX Symp. Networked Syst. Des. Implement.*, 2015, pp. 117–130.

[67] (2016). Project Clearwater. [Online]. Available: http://www.projectclearwater.org/about-clearwater/

[68] (2016). Welcome to SIPp. [Online]. Available: http://sipp.sourceforge.net/

[69] (2016). OpenStack Cloud Software. [Online]. Available: www.openstack.org

[70] P. Garg and Y.-S. Wang, "NVGRE: Network Virtualization using Generic Routing Encapsulation," 2014.

[71] R. Jones, "NetPerf: a network performance benchmark," *Inf. Networks Div. Hewlett-Packard Co.*, 1996.

[72] R. S. Roman Dementiev, Thomas Willhalm, Otto Bruggeman, Patrick Fay, Patrick Ungerer, Austen Ott, Patrick Lu, James Harris, Phil Kerly, Patrick Konsor, Andrey Semin, Michael Kanaly, Ryan Brazones, "Intel® Performance Counter Monitor - A better way to measure CPU utilization." .

[73] L. Subramanian, V. Seshadri, A. Ghosh, S. Khan, and O. Mutlu, "The Application Slowdown Model: Quantifying and Controlling the Impact of Inter-Application Interference at Shared Caches and Main Memory," in *Proc. of the 48th International Symposium on Microarchitecture, 2015, pp. 62-75.*

[74] O. Mutlu and T. Moscibroda, "Parallelism-aware batch scheduling: Enhancing both performance and fairness of shared DRAM systems," in *Proc. International Symposium on Computer Architecture*, 2008, pp. 63–74.

[75] L. Liu, Y. Li, Z. Cui, Y. Bao, M. Chen, and C. Wu, "Going vertical in memory management: Handling multiplicity by multi-policy," in *Proc. Int. Symp. Comput. Archit.*, 2014, pp. 169–180.

[76] M. Song, Y. Hu, Y. Xu, C. Li, H. Chen, J. Yuan, and T. Li, "Bridging the Semantic Gaps of GPU Acceleration for Scale-out CNN-based Big Data Processing: Think Big, See Small," in *Proc. of the 2016 International Conference on Parallel Architectures and Compilation*, 2016, pp. 315–326.

[77] Y. Zhang, M. A. Laurenzano, J. Mars, and L. Tang, "Smite: Precise qos prediction on real system smt processors to improve utilization in warehouse scale computers," in *Proc. of the 47th International Symposium on Microarchitecture,* 2014, pp. 406-418.

[78] (2016). Deutsche Telekom experimenting with NFV in Docker | Business Cloud News. [Online]. Available: http://www.businesscloudnews.com/2015/02/09/deutsche-telekom-experimenting-with-nfv-in-docker/

[79] Iain Morris. (2015). BT Pins NFV Future on Containerization. [Online]. Available: http://www.lightreading.com/nfv/nfv-strategies/bt-pins-nfv-future-on-containerizatio n/d/d-id/718920

[80] E. Jeong, S. Wood, M. Jamshed, H. Jeong, S. Ihm, D. Han, and K. Park, "mTCP: a Highly Scalable User-level TCP Stack for Multicore Systems," in *Proc. 11th USENIX Symp. Networked Syst. Des. Implement.*, 2014, pp. 489–502.

[81] X. Jiang, Y. Solihin, L. Zhao, and R. Iyer, "Architecture support for improving bulk memory copying and initialization performance," in *Proc. Parallel Archit. Compil. Tech. Conf.*, 2009, pp. 169–180.

[82] X. Xiang, B. Bao, C. Ding, and Y. Gao, "Linear-time modeling of program working set in shared cache," in *Proc. Parallel Archit. Compil. Tech. Conf.*, 2011, pp. 350–360.

[83] X. Xiang, C. Ding, H. Luo, and B. Bao, "HOTL: A Higher Order Theory of Locality," in *Proc. of the Eighteenth International Conference on Architectural Support for Programming Languages and Operating Systems*, 2013, pp. 343–356.

[84] X. Hu, X. Wang, Y. Li, L. Zhou, Y. Luo, C. Ding, S. Jiang, and Z. Wang, "LAMA: Optimized Locality-aware Memory Allocation for Key-value Cache," in *Proc. 2015 USENIX Annual Technical Conference*, 2015, pp. 57–69.

[85] C. A. Waldspurger, N. Park, A. Garthwaite, and I. Ahmad, "Efficient MRC Construction with SHARDS," in *Proc. 13th USENIX Conference on File and Storage Technologies*, 2015, pp. 95–110.

[86] D. Merkel, "Docker: lightweight linux containers for consistent development and deployment," *Linux J.*, vol. 2014, no. 239, p. 2, 2014.

[87] Oprofile. [Online]. Available: http://oprofile.sourceforge.net/

[88] X. Ding, K. Wang, and X. Zhang, "SRM-buffer: An OS Buffer Management Technique to Prevent Last Level Cache from Thrashing in Multicores," in *Proc. of the Sixth Conference on Computer Systems*, 2011, pp. 243–256.

[89] X. Hu, X. Wang, L. Zhou, Y. Luo, C. Ding, and Z. Wang, "Kinetic Modeling of Data Eviction in Cache," in *Proc. 2016 USENIX Annual Technical Conference*, 2016, pp. 351–364.

[90] L. Zhao, S. Makineni, R. Illikkal, R. Iyer, and L. Bhuyan, "Efficient Caching Techniques for Server Network Acceleration," in *Proc. Advanced Networking and Communications Hardware Workshop*, 2004.

[91] Y. Jiang, E. Z. Zhang, K. Tian, and X. Shen, "Is reuse distance applicable to data locality analysis on chip multiprocessors?," in *Proc. International Conference on Compiler Construction*, 2010, pp. 264–282.

[92] X. Xiang, B. Bao, C. Ding, and K. Shen, "Cache conscious task regrouping on multicore processors," in *Proc. 12th IEEE/ACM Int. Symp. Clust. Cloud Grid Comput.*, 2012, pp. 603–611.

[93] X. Xiang, B. Bao, T. Bai, C. Ding, and T. Chilimbi, "All-window Profiling and Composable Models of Cache Sharing," in *Proc. of the 16th ACM Symposium on Principles and Practice of Parallel Programming*, 2011, pp. 91–102.

[94] A. V Goldberg, "An Efficient Implementation of a Scaling Minimum-Cost Flow Algorithm," *J. Algorithms*, vol. 22, no. 1, pp. 1–29, 1997.

[95] J. Lin, Q. Lu, X. Ding, Z. Zhang, X. Zhang, and P. Sadayappan, "Gaining insights into multicore cache partitioning: Bridging the gap between simulation and real systems," in *Proc. International Symposium on High-Performance Computer Architecture*, 2008, pp. 367–378.

BIOGRAPHICAL SKETCH

Yang Hu was born in Baotou, China in June of 1985. He was enrolled in Tianjin University, China in 2003 and received his B.S. degree in electrical engineering in 2007. He was enrolled in Tsinghua University, China in 2008 and received his M.S. degree in micro and nano-electronic engineering in 2011.He began to pursue his Ph.D. degree in Department of Electrical and Computer Engineering at the University of Florida in the fall semester, 2011. He obtained his M.S. degree in Dec, 2016 and his Ph.D. degree in Aug, 2017. He is a recipient of the prestigious Graduate Alumni Fellowship at the University of Florida. His research interests include data center scale computing, sustainable computing, power/energy management, architectural support for network function virtualization, and heterogeneous architectural support for deep learning. He has published over ten papers at top-tier conferences including ISCA, MICRO, HPCA, ASPLOS, PACT, DSN, ICS, etc. His research has been recognized with best paper awards at IEEE CAL 2015 and best paper nominee at HPCA 2017.